HOPE RESTORED
THE FIGHT AGAINST CHILD LABOUR

DR. SHAILENDRA PANDYA

BLUEROSE PUBLISHERS
India | U.K.

Copyright © Dr. Shailendra Pandya 2025

All rights reserved by author. No part of this publication may be reproduced, stored in a retrieval system or transmitted in any form or by any means, electronic, mechanical, photocopying, recording or otherwise, without the prior permission of the author. Although every precaution has been taken to verify the accuracy of the information contained herein, the publisher assume no responsibility for any errors or omissions. No liability is assumed for damages that may result from the use of information contained within.

BlueRose Publishers takes no responsibility for any damages, losses, or liabilities that may arise from the use or misuse of the information, products, or services provided in this publication.

For permissions requests or inquiries regarding this publication, please contact:

BLUEROSE PUBLISHERS
www.BlueRoseONE.com
info@bluerosepublishers.com
+91 8882 898 898
+4407342408967

ISBN: 978-93-7018-904-1

Cover design: Daksh
Typesetting: Tanya Raj Upadhyay

First Edition: June 2025

प्रधान मंत्री
Prime Minister

New Delhi
वैशाख 04, शक संवत 1947
17th April 2025

Dear Dr. Shailendra Pandya,

It is a matter of great pride and inspiration to witness the remarkable work of Dr. Shailendra Pandya, a distinguished child rights specialist and former member of the Rajasthan State Commission for Protection of Child Rights. For the past 15 years, Dr. Pandya has been tirelessly dedicated to the rescue, rehabilitation, and empowerment of children engaged in labour across India.

His efforts have directly led to the rescue of more than 1,000 children from exploitative conditions, offering them a new path filled with hope, dignity, and opportunity. Dr. Pandya's deep experience and on-ground understanding have immensely contributed to shaping policies and strengthening the efforts of the government and other stakeholders committed to child protection.

This book reflects not only his personal journey and commitment but also serves as a powerful resource and guide for everyone working to end child labour in India. I extend my heartfelt best wishes to Dr. Pandya and to Gayatri Seva Sansthan, Udaipur, for their continued dedication and invaluable contributions toward building a safer and more just world for our children.

With deep respect and appreciation,

(Narendra Modi)

Dr. Shailendra Pandya,
3-DHA-1, Hiran Magri, Sector-5, Prabhat Nagar,
Udaipur, Rajasthan 313002

Acknowledgment

Whether it is a book or a chapter of life, no matter how it is written, the journey to its final form is never one carried out alone. More than the writer, it is often those unseen individuals who may not have penned a single word in the book but whose inspiration, strength, teachings and support breathe life into every sentence.

While I have previously authored several guidelines, SOPs and Handbooks, this book truly marks a personal milestone. I am deeply grateful to everyone whose direct or indirect support made it possible for me to write this book.

With reverence, I bow to *Ved Mata Gayatri*, and express my deepest respect and gratitude to my father and eternal source of inspiration, **Shri Laxmi Narayan Pandya**, and my mother **Smt. Kalpana Pandya**, whose lives of selfless service, values, and compassion have constantly energized and guided me. Without their unwavering support and blessings, my journey from engineering into the field of social work would not have been possible. Also, it is with great pleasure and a deep sense of privilege to have received the blessings of **Shri Narendra Modi Ji**, Hon'ble Prime Minister of India, for this endeavour.

As I reflect on the past sixteen years, I vividly recall the faces of those who have walked this path with me, offering courage, wisdom and direction. I fondly remember my first meeting in 2010 with **Shri Sanjay Kumar Nirala, and Smt. Sulagna Roy**, which marked my initial step into the field of child protection.

I am deeply grateful to **Dr. Mahaveer Jain**, the then Senior Fellow at V.V. Giri National Labour Institute, Government of India; **Dr. Sharad Chandra Purohit**, former Director of Rajasthan SIERT and then Chairperson of Gayatri Seva Sansthan; **Shri S.L. Bohra (Retd. I.A.S), Former Collector & Distt. Magistrate**; **Dr. T.C. Damor, (Retd. I.P.S) Ex I.G. Police and Ex - Vice Chancellor**; **Dr. Rajkumari Bhargava**, a dedicated academician and **Shri Chetan Pandey,** CEO, Gayatri Seva Sansthan. Their training, insights, and encouragement have left a lasting imprint on my journey.

A defining moment came in 2014, when the Nobel Peace Prize was awarded to India's revered Child Rights Activist, **Shri Kailash Satyarthi.** That singular event sparked a renewed passion and deeper commitment in me for the cause. Kailash Ji continues to remain a guiding light and a source of inspiration.

In 2016, I was given the opportunity by **Smt. Manan Chaturvedi**, the then Chairperson of the Rajasthan State Commission for Protection of Child Rights, to work on child rights at the policy level with the state government. Since then, I have had the privilege of contributing across three successive administrations. I sincerely thank **Smt. Vasundhara Raje, Shri Ashok**

Gehlot, and Shri Bhajan Lal Sharma for enabling these meaningful experiences.

I would also like to express heartfelt gratitude to **Shri Priyank Kanoongo**, then Chairperson of the National Commission for Protection of Child Rights and now a Member of the National Human Rights Commission, Government of India. His guidance in national and inter-state child labour rescue cases has been invaluable.

I extend my sincere gratitude to **Shri Bhuvan Ribhu,** founder of the *Just Rights for Children Alliance*, whose constant encouragement and collaboration have been a continuous source of inspiration in my efforts to combat child labour.

With deep emotion, I also wish to acknowledge **Shri Ravi Kant, Shri Rajeev Bhardwaj**, and **Shri Bidhan Chandra** from *Access to Justice*, whose mentorship and guidance have been like that of caring guardians on this journey. I am also deeply thankful for the networks and alliances I was privileged to be a part of, which gave me invaluable opportunities to learn, particularly the Just Rights for Children Alliance, the Resource Group on Child Rights in Rajasthan (RG-CRiR), and the Rajasthan Child Advisory Group (R-CAG).

I extend special appreciation to our entire team at *Gayatri Seva Sansthan, Udaipur,* and especially **Ms. Ashita Jain,** my dedicated colleague, whose unwavering efforts played a vital role in turning the dream of my first published book into reality.

Finally, I extend my heartfelt gratitude to my friend, partner, and beloved wife **Aditi**, and my dear daughter **Shailja**, whose faith in me during every rescue operation and moment of doubt has been a constant source of strength and energy.

Thank you all for walking with me on this journey. This book is not just mine, it is ours.

Preface

I find myself writing this book at a time when the noise of progress, power, and global ambition fills the air. Every nation is on a quest to grow faster, stand taller, and claim its place in the world. This collective momentum is powerful. But in the midst of these roaring conversations, I often pause and listen for a quieter voice. I wonder what do the children of these nations dream of ? Do they find themselves reflected in the shining mirrors of development we hold up so proudly?

Having worked in the field of child protection for over a decade, I have stood on both sides, where policies are drafted in high-ceiling rooms, and where barefoot children wait in silence, hoping someone would notice. I have looked into the eyes of children whose innocence stands on fragile ground, threatened by poverty, abuse, and the quiet cruelty of neglect. In a country like India, where nearly half of the population is below the age of 18, the soul of our development cannot be measured in GDP alone, it must be seen in the safety, dignity, and happiness of every child.

So I ask can we do it? Can we rise above the noise to truly listen to the needs of our children? Can we shield them from the new-age dangers that come with rapid technological shifts, social isolation, and widening gaps between the rich and the poor? My answer is a resounding yes. And it is this unwavering belief that led me to write this book.

Within these pages, I have attempted to weave together moments, some painful, some hopeful from my journey. These are stories of children who have faced odds far beyond their years, and of everyday heroes who chose to act. These stories are not just about suffering, they are about strength. Not just about darkness but also the sparks of light that shine through.

This book is for many. For those who are just beginning to understand child labour, for the young ones whose hearts are filled with questions and compassion, and for adults who are willing to look beyond their routines to see the invisible battles being fought by millions of children every day. Whether you are a teacher, a student, a policymaker, a parent, or simply someone who cares—this book is for you. It serves as a practical guide to understanding child labour from identification and rescue to the entire process of rehabilitation. These insights come from my real-life experiences in the field and the lessons learned on the ground.

When I first sat down to write, I was hesitant. How can words possibly carry the weight of a child's silence? How can ink reflect the fear in their eyes, the strength in their quiet resilience? I do not know if I have succeeded. But I do know this, if even one story in this book stirs a conversation, a question, or a commitment in your heart, then the purpose is served.

Because protecting our children is not a task for one person or one government. It is a collective calling. It is not only about drafting laws, it is about compassion, action, and the refusal to look away.

And maybe, just by walking together on this path, we can build a world where every child not only feels safe but stands tall with pride, because children are not only our tomorrow, they are our today. They are the present, the living pulse of the nation.

— Dr. Shailendra Pandya

Table of Contents

Child Labour: The Burning Issue 1

Chapter 1: A Small Beginning 9

Identification 14

Chapter 2: Finding the Invisible Children....................15

Chapter 3: Eyes on the Ground: The Power of Local Committees 21

Forming of Teams 30

Chapter 4: The Convergence Model............................31

Conducting Rescues 39

Chapter 5: The Moving Train: Beyond the Plan 40

Chapter 6: Baal Swaraj - Beyond Borders 47

Chapter 7: Bonded Childhood......................................56

Registering First Information Report (FIR)......................66

Chapter 08: Model FIR 67

Medical, Age Determination, Counseling & Shelter.........73

Chapter 09: Age Matters..74

Rehabilitation...83

Chapter 10: Rescue is Only the beginning...................84

Follow Up 91

Chapter 11: The Final Step 92

Chapter 12: Restoring Hope..102

Child Labour: The Burning Issue

Child labour remains a persistent problem in the world today. The latest global estimates indicate that 160 million children – 63 million girls and 97 million boys – were in child labour globally at the beginning of 2020, accounting for almost 1 in 10 of all children worldwide. Seventy-nine million children – nearly half of all those in child labour – were in hazardous work that directly endangers their health, safety and moral development.

Global progress against child labour has stagnated since 2016. The percentage of children in child labour remained unchanged over the four-year period while the absolute number of children in child labour increased by over 8 million. Similarly, the percentage of children in hazardous work was almost unchanged but rose in absolute terms by 6.5 million children. The global picture continues to progress against child labour in Asia, the Pacific, Latin America and the Caribbeans. In both regions, child labour trend went downward over the last four years in percentage and absolute terms.

Similar progress in Sub-Saharan Africa has proven elusive. This region has seen an increase in both the number and percentage of children in child labour since 2012. There are now more children in child labour in sub-Saharan Africa than in the rest of the world combined. Global child labour goals will not be achieved without a breakthrough in this region. Continued progress was registered over the last four years among children aged 12 to 14 and 15 to 17. Child labour in both age groups declined in percentage and absolute terms, continuing a consistent downward trend seen in previous estimates. Child labour rose among young children aged 5 to 11, however, after the 2016 global estimates signaled slowing progress for this age group. There were 16.8 million more children aged 5 to 11 in child labour in 2020 than in 2016.

The COVID-19 further threatened to erode global progress against child labour unless urgent mitigation measures are taken. An analysis suggested that by the end of 2022, 8.9 million children would have entered the workforce as child labourers due to rising poverty driven by the pandemic.

Yet the predicted additional rise in child labour is by no means a foregone conclusion. The actual impact will depend on policy responses. Two additional scenarios demonstrate the huge influence of social protection coverage on child labour in the near term. Where social protection coverage is allowed to slip, a significant further increase in child labour.

Key Findings

Involvement in child labour is higher for boys than girls at all ages. Among all boys, 11.2 percent are in child labour compared to 7.8 per cent of all girls. In absolute numbers, boys in child labour outnumber girls by 34 million. When the definition of child labour expands to include household chores for 21 hours or more each week, the gender gap in prevalence among boys and girls aged 5 to 14 is reduced by almost half.

Child labour is much more common in rural areas. There are 122.7 million rural children in child labour compared to 37.3 million urban children. The prevalence of child labour in rural areas (13.9 per cent) is close to three times higher than in urban areas (4.7 per cent).

Most child labour – for boys and girls alike – continues to occur in agriculture. Seventy per cent of all children in child labour, 112 million children in total, are in agriculture. Many are younger children, underscoring agriculture as an entry point to child labour. Over three quarters of all children aged 5 to 11 in child labour work in agriculture.

The largest share of child labour takes place within families. Seventy-two per cent of all child labour and 83 per cent of child labour among children aged 5 to 11 occurs within families, primarily on family farms or in family micro-enterprises. Family-based child labour is frequently hazardous despite common perceptions of the family as offering a safer work environment. More than one in four children aged 5 to 11 and nearly half of children aged 12 to 14 in family-based child labour are in work likely to harm their health, safety or morals.

Child labour is frequently associated with children being out of school. A large share of younger children in child labour are excluded from school despite falling within the age range for compulsory education. More than a quarter of children aged 5 to 11 and over a third of children aged 12 to 14 who are in child labour are out of school. This severely constrains their prospects for decent work in youth and adulthood as well as their life potential overall. Many more children in child labour struggle to balance the demands of school and child labour at the same time, which compromises their education and their right to leisure.

CHILD LABOUR IN THE GLOBAL DEVELOPMENT AGENDA

SDG TARGET 8.7: Take immediate and effective measures to eradicate forced labour, end modern slavery and human trafficking and secure the prohibition and elimination of the worst forms of child labour, including recruitment and use of child soldiers, and by 2025 end child labour in all its forms.

The international community has recognized the importance of ending child labour as part of achieving SDG 8 on decent work and economic growth. Under this goal, target 8.7 is to end child labour in all its forms by 2025.

Ending child labour will also contribute to progress on many other SDGs, especially on education and health.

In INDIA, THERE ARE 10.1 MILLION WORKING CHILDREN BETWEEN THE AGE OF 5-14 (CENSUS, 2011)

As per Census 2011, the total child population in India in the age group (5-14) years is 259.6 million. Of these, 10.1 million (3.9% of total child population) are working, either as 'main worker' or as 'marginal worker'. In addition, more than 42.7 million children in India are out of school.

The number of child workers has increased in urban areas, indicating the growing demand for child workers in menial jobs. Child labour has different ramifications in both rural and urban India.

Year	Percentage of working children (5-14)			Total number of working children (5-14) (in millions)		
	Rural	Urban	Total	Rural	Urban	Total
2001	5.9	2.1	5	11.4	1.3	12.7
2011	4.3	2.9	3.9	8.1	2	10.1

*Source – Census 2001 and 2011

Distribution of working children by type of work in 2011

Area of work	Percentage	Numbers (in millions)
Cultivators	26.0	2.63
Agricultural labourers	32.9	3.33
Household industry workers	5.2	0.52
Other workers	35.8	3.62

*Source – Census 2011

Note: 'Other workers': Workers other than cultivators, agricultural labourers or workers in household industries

Together, Uttar Pradesh, Bihar, Rajasthan, Maharashtra, and Madhya Pradesh constitute nearly 55% of total working children in India.

States	Percentage	Numbers (In million)
Uttar Pradesh	21.5	2.18
Bihar	10.7	1.09
Rajasthan	8.4	0.85
Maharashtra	7.2	0.73
Madhya Pradesh	6.9	0.70

*Source – Census 2011

Now that we have spoken about the urgent need to address the issue of child labour and why it is imperative to act, let us turn our focus to the process of saving a childhood. The rescue of a child is not just a physical act—it is the beginning of restoring dignity, dreams, and freedom. A child can be saved through coordinated efforts involving legal intervention, rehabilitation, and education. Timely implementation of laws like the POCSO Act and the proposed anti-trafficking Bill plays a crucial role. Equally important is the role of civil society, movements, and compassionate individuals who stand up for children's rights. Every rescued child must be given access to quality education, psychological care, and opportunities for a better future. Saving a childhood is a shared responsibility. It begins with awareness, grows with action, and culminates in giving back to children what they truly deserve, a safe, free, and joyful life.

Sl. No.	Name of State/UT	No. of working children in the age group of 5-14 years	
		Census 2001	Census 2011
1	Uttar Pradesh	1927997	896301
2	Andhra Pradesh	1363339	404851
3	Rajasthan	1262570	252338
4	Bihar	1117500	451590
5	Madhya Pradesh	1065259	286310
6	West Bengal	857087	234275
7	Karnataka	822615	249432
8	Maharashtra	764075	496916
9	Gujarat	485530	250318
10	Tamil Nadu	418801	151437
11	Jharkhand	407200	90996
12	Odisha	377594	92087

13	Chhattisgarh	364572	63884
14	Assam	351416	99512
15	Haryana	253491	53492
16	Punjab	177268	90353
17	Jammu & Kashmir	175630	25528
18	Himachal Pradesh	107774	15001
19	Uttarakhand	70183	28098
20	Meghalaya	53940	18839
21	Nagaland	45874	11062
22	Delhi U.T.	41899	26473
23	Manipur	28836	11805
24	Mizoram	26265	2793
25	Kerala	26156	21757
26	Tripura	21756	4998
27	Arunachal Pradesh	18482	5766
28	Sikkim	16457	2704
29	Dadra & Nagar H.	4274	1054
30	Goa	4138	6920
31	Chandigarh U.T.	3779	3135
32	Andaman & Nicobar Island	1960	999
33	Pondicherry U.T.	1904	1421
34	Daman & Diu U.T.	729	774
35	Lakshadweep UT	27	28

Chapter 1:
A Small Beginning

It's often the simplest places that leave the deepest marks on us. I was born in Udaipur city, often called the City of Lakes. It's a place where history breathes through its palaces and where culture runs as deep as the waters of Lake Pichola. Growing up there inevitably meant being surrounded by grandeur and heritage. Udaipur shaped my early world—a blend of tradition and change; of ancient roots and unfolding possibilities.

My father, Shri Laxmi Narayan Pandya, was aware of the weight of struggle from a young age. Walking barefoot for miles to attend school wasn't a hardship for him; it was a path toward something greater. Through sheer grit and determination, he secured a place in the banking sector. In our community, that revered more than just a stable job. It meant breaking barriers. But for him, success was never meant to end with personal achievement. His dreams always had a place for others. Eventually, he chose to leave his government job. Deep within, he carried a conviction. He had been fortunate to receive an education, but what about the countless children who hadn't? Someone needed to mediate that gap, and that belief became his purpose. He founded Gayatri Shiksha Sansthan in Udaipur city, now known as Gayatri Seva Sansthan, starting small with a simple aim of educating children from all walks of life.

Whatever surplus the school generated, he used to run a free school in tribal areas. That was his way of giving back, his way of serving those who needed it most.

Beside my father, always, was my mother, Kalpana. She was the quiet strength that steadied our home. Never loud, never demanding, but always there like the ground beneath your feet. She taught me that true courage doesn't announce itself. It simply carries on.

In our home, education wasn't forced, it was celebrated. It meant freedom. The kind that lets you choose, speak and become. Drawn to problem-solving, I chose engineering. I liked how coding made me think and create. College was full of computers, classes, and friends. I was headed toward a stable, well-paid career. A software engineer. Life, as they say, was on track.

Until it wasn't.

In my third year of engineering, I got placed at an MNC. That's often the moment of relief for many students. The final year tends to be less intense, a space to breathe, to explore. And that's exactly what I decided to do. Rather than travel to faraway cities, I thought, why not look more closely at what's around us?

That thought led me back to the tribal belt near our region. Villages I'd only heard about now became real. The first time I truly saw village life up close, it wasn't the hardships that struck me, but the grace of it. Simple homes, shared meals, quiet laughter. People had little in terms of wealth, but there was no shortage of love, dignity, and dreams.

During my visits to rural and tribal regions, I often found myself in conversation with the locals. One of those interactions that stood out for me was when I met a boy who told me he was in 10th standard. When I asked what he was studying, he said he had just given his 10th board exam. I asked about his future plans. He replied casually, "Ab kamane jaunga." When I asked why, he simply said, "Yaha toh sab jaate hai." ("To earn… everyone goes here.")

It wasn't said with sadness. It was just a fact. As normal to him as school was to me. And that shook me.

It was the ordinariness of it. The quiet acceptance. Children, still in school, preparing not for exams, but for labour. He spoke of going to Ahmedabad to earn. That stayed with me. His words stirred something inside me, and over the next few days, I began noticing more. Young boys washing dishes at roadside stalls, tending shops, lifting loads in markets. They were called Chhotus. Their childhoods were fading, quietly, without protest.

Something about it all felt deeply wrong.

And then, one evening, I returned to the city. Restless, I began surfing TV channels, and a scene from the movie *Swades* played by Shah Rukh Khan standing by a water pump in a village. I paused my search for channels there and that very moment hit me hard. I just sat there. The message was simple, but it echoed deeply. What if the answers we chase in big cities already exist in the roots we leave behind?

That night, sleep never came.

The next morning, I told my father, "I want to do something for children."

He listened, then asked gently, "How will you do it?"

I had no plan. No grand vision. Just a stirring inside that refused to quiet down.

And so, I followed it.

That decision marked the start of a journey I could never have predicted. I left behind code to pursue the cause. I enrolled in a post-graduate course in social work, studying while also gaining field knowledge, both hand in hand. Later, I took up a Ph.D. in child rights.

The path was not easy, but it felt right. Every challenge seemed to have a reason. Every step forward felt like a return to purpose, to roots, to something bigger than myself.

In those early days, I often wondered whether one person could really make a difference.

From coding computers to protecting childhoods.
From solving problems on a screen to solving them in the streets.

This was just the beginning.

What followed was my journey into the field of child protection, driven by a single aim of freeing our nation from the curse of child labour. Slowly, I started to understand the system, the challenges, and the small steps that could make a difference. Over time, through hands-on experiences and learning in the field, I began to grasp the process of rescuing children involved in labour. In the chapters ahead, I'll be sharing the step-by- step journey with you. Not as an expert, but as someone who has been learning along the way, hoping it might be useful to someone who wants to understand or take part in this work too.

Identification

Chapter 2:
Finding the Invisible Children

The decision to deepen my understanding of child protection in India did not begin in a classroom. I believed in education, yes, but I knew no amount of reading could replace the lessons waiting in the dusty lanes and hidden corners of our villages, where children lived and toiled, far from policy papers and perfect plans.

From the very beginning, my mission was clear: to reach the children trapped in labour and trafficking. But one cannot protect what one refuses to notice. And the worst part is that these millions of children were not invisible but hidden in plain sight.

So I began to travel. I rode my bike through landscapes that shifted from traffic to the tilled earth. Towns faded into paths, paths into trails.

At first glance, it all seemed idyllic. Men guiding wooden ploughs through rich soil, women in vibrant saris moving with grace, fields stretching endlessly beneath the sun. But then I began to see. A girl no older than ten rocking her baby brother under a low roof. A boy with soapy hands scrubbing tea cups. Children herding goats barefoot instead of reciting lessons. School bags replaced by sacks. Pencils traded for ploughs.

Once I noticed them, I couldn't stop seeing them. They were everywhere. Their invisibility wasn't a trick of the eye. It was a symptom of the system. These children had been consumed by responsibilities too heavy for their years. They had become caretakers, labourers, and providers.

In those early days, every ride into a new village became a lesson. Some moments lifted me, a wave from a curious child, a smile breaking through caution. Others stayed heavy, a boy shrinking away, unsure if I was a friend or just another adult passing by.

I learned that child labour doesn't always wear the face of misery. Sometimes it looks like duty. Sometimes like tradition. But it is still a theft, theft of time, of dreams, and of the future.

Observation became my greatest tool. Listening, my strongest strategy. I began to connect the dots: how poverty, migration, lack of education, and exploitation formed a web that held children in place.

In 15 years of working with children, I've learned that there are critical steps that must come before rescue. The key lies in quick and timely identification.

Here are some of the ideal processes I've come to trust.

First, **understand the local context.** You cannot parachute into a village and expect to make change. You have to become part of it. You must see what others do not, and do so with care and confidentiality.

Your purpose cannot be to simply rescue. It must be to help people recognize the value of their children's time.

Often, parents, employers, and even the children themselves may be frightened or confused by your presence. Social workers must build trust. Sometimes, connecting families to social security schemes is the bridge. These schemes become proof that alternatives are possible.

Next comes **identifying the risk**. This means not just seeing a child working, but mapping the ecosystem around them. Who is the trafficker? Who brought the child? What are the industries that absorb them? You start connecting names, locations, and seasonal patterns—understanding not just the act, but the entire system.

In my career I have remembered several times tracking a whole network—local contractors, industry agents, even village-level enablers. The information didn't come from officials. It came from village youth committees, from school children, and from relationships patiently built.

That's why **building a strong local network** is non-negotiable. The network becomes your early warning system. Many times, I heard about children being taken away not through headlines, but through the network.

I often used tools like the **Identification of Children in Need of Care and Protection (CNCP), an abstract** survey system designed to capture vital details. Even in small areas, this tool helped me record patterns: names, ages, type of work, location, first sighting. Over time, we could map which children needed urgent care, who had dropped out of school, and who might be trafficked next.

S. No.	Place	Nature of work	Approx. Age	Interstate/ within state

Cross-verification is a crucial step in ensuring that the children identified in the initial interaction are truly in need of rescue. It helps confirm the accuracy of your observations and prevents premature action. Sometimes, the signs of child labour are subtle—children may not be attending school regularly, might just seem like helping out at the local shop nearby, or may move in and out of villages at unusual hours. These situations may seem harmless at first glance but could be masking deeper risks.

It is important not to act on first impressions unless the situation is urgent. Begin by observing carefully and discreetly. Take notes, and if appropriate, capture photos or short videos for documentation, always keeping the child's safety and privacy in mind. Revisit the location after a day or two to see if the child is still engaged in the same work. This repetition helps you build a clearer picture.

Before taking any action, review the situation thoroughly. Ask yourself: What kind of work is the child doing? How long has this been going on? What risks is the child exposed to? Are other children involved, or is there an employer or trafficker behind the scenes?

Only when these questions have been answered should you proceed with a rescue. Cross-verification ensures that interventions are accurate, thoughtful, and truly protective. It helps avoid the risks of rescuing the wrong child, or acting without the proper support systems in place.

This is how we make sure that the right children are rescued, at the right time, for the right reasons. And throughout all of this, never forget: child labour is not an accident. It is a system. One that's convenient, invisible, and profitable.

You'll find a boy handing you tea with practiced speed. A girl threading a needle in a dusty backroom. They don't complain. But that doesn't mean they're free.

These dusty rides into rural India became my education; the children, my teachers.

And in their silence, I found my mission.

Highlights

This chapter explores one of the most crucial yet often overlooked aspects of combating child labour and trafficking, the process of identification. Before any rescue can take place, it is essential to recognize and understand the realities children face. The journey begins not in offices or policy rooms, but on the ground, by paying attention to those children who are hidden in plain sight. Many are engaged in labour under the pretext of helping their families, making their exploitation harder to detect and easier to dismiss. The chapter outlines five key steps in this identification process that ensures that rescue is not just reactive, but informed, timely, and truly effective.

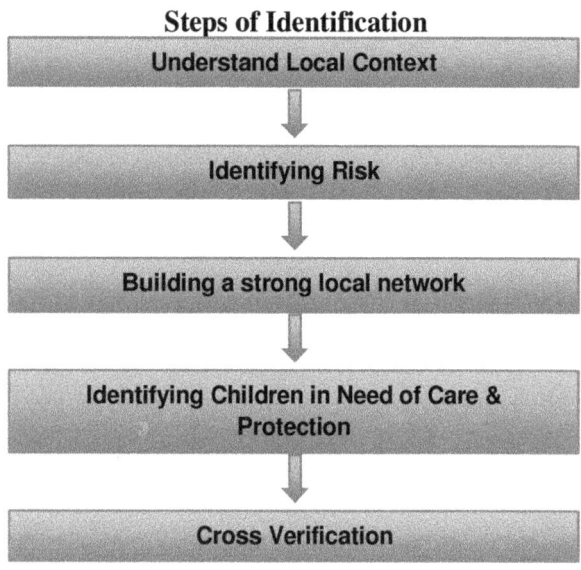

Steps of Identification
- Understand Local Context
- Identifying Risk
- Building a strong local network
- Identifying Children in Need of Care & Protection
- Cross Verification

Chapter 3:
Eyes on the Ground: The Power of Local Committees

In my earlier chapter, I spoke about how essential it is to build networks that can respond swiftly and sensitively to child protection issues. This chapter is a continuation of that belief, a lived example of what happens when community structures begin to see through the right lens.

When I first began working in the field, I carried one firm belief: I could not do this alone. Protecting children is not the work of an individual. It requires the strength of a collective. It needs systems and committees that do not just exist on paper but that breathe and respond. These structures already exist under the Integrated Child Protection Scheme, in the form of Panchayat and Block Level Child Protection Committees. But forming a committee is one thing. Activating it is another.

In my years of fieldwork, I focused on this very gap. Through regular training, dialogues, and continuous engagement, I worked to bring these committees to life. Slowly and steadily, they began to function with purpose.

This story comes from Nathara village in the Sarada Block of Salumber District. A village like many others, with scattered homes, winding paths, and quiet afternoons. But what happened here was extraordinary, because here, the system worked.

After one such training session, a call came to me from members of the Panchayat Level Child Protection Committee. "Now that you've shown us this lens," one of them said, "we think there's a child-headed family in the village."

I listened closely. The details were vague, but the urgency was clear. Three children. Father died. Mother ran off. An elder brother who was said to be working in the city and sending money home. The younger siblings were surviving alone.

Without delay, I along with the then Additional Director, Child Rights Department Ms. Meena Sharma and then Child Welfare Committee Udaipur Chairperson Mr. Dhruv Kumar Kaviya went to Nathara.

The house was small and fragile, barely holding itself together. Inside were three children, Lali, Suresh, and Radha (name changed) aged just 13, 8, 10. Their clothes were worn thin, and their eyes were quieter than they should be. The elder brother, Ramesh, was not there. He had gone to the city to work, they said. He would send money whenever he could. They had not heard from him in days.

We managed to trace a contact number, and after several attempts, we spoke to Ramesh. He was hesitant at first, unsure of who we were and what we wanted.

But slowly and gently, we explained: his siblings were safe, and now, it was time for him to be safe too.

We coordinated with local authorities and brought him back from the city, where he had been working under exploitative conditions and barely surviving. He was just thirteen.

When all four children stood together again, something shifted. Not just in their eyes, but in the hearts of everyone around. It was not just about removing them from risk. It was about restoring their right to live, to laugh, and to learn.

This case reminded me once again that identification is not a passive act. It is active, intentional, and often collective. When child protection structures are equipped with the right understanding, they become powerful. In Nathara, the PLCPC did not wait for a formal complaint. They saw. They acted. And because of that, four children were saved—one from labour, and three from neglect.

The Juvenile Justice Act lays down clear responsibilities. Abandonment is a crime. Neglect is a crime. Children found alone or exploited must be presented to the Child Welfare Committee within 24 hours. But these laws mean little unless they are animated by human vigilance.

All 4 siblings were taken to a child care institution. They received not just food, shelter, and education, but also dignity. Their laughter was not just a sound. It was a signal. That rescue had worked. That restoration had begun. And that it all started because someone noticed.

Highlights

The disconnect between policy-making and on-the-ground realities can have serious consequences for children. The story serves as a stark reminder of the dangers children face when vulnerability and neglect go unnoticed. It highlights the critical role of activating the child protection committees, legal safeguards, and collaborative efforts in protecting children. The successful rehabilitation of the siblings demonstrates the profound impact of timely intervention, the importance of building trust, and the vital role of care systems in restoring a child's right to safety, education, and hope. The journey of these four siblings is not just one of rescue but it serves as a powerful testament to the fragility of childhood when protective systems fail, and the strength of our collective action when they succeed. Legal protections, such as the JJ Act, must be paired with proactive tools like vulnerability mapping and the vigilance of community networks to ensure no child is left behind. When communities are informed and engaged, and when laws are enforced with empathy and urgency, we don't just save children, we empower them to dream.

Children in Need of Care and Protection (CNCP): Definition and Legal Provisions under the Juvenile Justice (Care and Protection of Children) Act, 2015

Definition:

According to **Section 2(14)** of the Juvenile Justice (Care and Protection of Children) Act, 2015, *Children in Need of Care and Protection* include, but are not limited to:

- Orphaned, abandoned, or surrendered children.
- Children without any visible means of subsistence or support.
- Victims of abuse, neglect, cruelty, or exploitation.
- Children who are at imminent risk of being trafficked or forced into Labour.
- Children found working in contravention of Labour laws.
- Children who are mentally or physically challenged, infected with HIV/AIDS, or suffering from terminal illnesses without support.

- Children living on the streets or in unsafe environments.

Key Safeguarding Provisions:

1. **Immediate Rescue and Production Before CWC**:
    - Children identified as CNCP must be produced before the **Child Welfare Committee (CWC)** within **24 hours**.
    - The **Special Juvenile Police Unit (SJPU)** or local police is responsible for ensuring this process.
    - Child Helpline - 1098
    - Non-Governmental Organizations
    - Any other person

2. **Emergency Care and Shelter**:
    - Provision for placing children in **Child Care Institutions (CCIs) or fit facilities/persons** for safety, health care, and rehabilitation.

3. **Individual Care Plans (ICPs)**:
    - Each child is entitled to a **customized care plan**, ensuring proper education, healthcare, counseling, and emotional support.

4. **Rehabilitation and Social Integration**:
    - Focus on **family-based care**, adoption (if necessary), or reintegration with extended family wherever possible.

5. **No Detention Policy**:
    - CNCPs are never to be held in police lock-ups or jails; they must be treated with compassion and dignity.

6. **Legal Aid and Counseling**:
    - Free **legal support and psychological counseling** must be provided.

7. **Role of CWC**:
    - The CWC has powers equivalent to that of a bench of magistrates and is the sole authority to decide on protective and rehabilitative measures for CNCPs.

Importance of Vulnerability Mapping in Preventing Child Labour and Trafficking

What is Vulnerability Mapping?

Vulnerability Mapping is a systematic process of identifying at-risk children and families based on socio-economic, geographic, and environmental indicators. It involves:

- Locating children out of school, orphaned, or working.

- Identifying families in extreme poverty, substance abuse, or migration-prone communities.
- Recognizing areas with history or patterns of child trafficking, bonded labour, or sexual exploitation.

Why is it Effective?

1. **Early Identification and Prevention**:
    - Helps locate children *before* they fall into exploitation, allowing for **preventive action** rather than reactive rescue.

2. **Targeted Interventions**:
    - Enables NGOs, schools, and local authorities to **focus resources** on the most vulnerable areas and children.

3. **Data-Driven Policy Making**:
    - Facilitates **evidence-based decisions** for child protection programs and budget allocations.

4. **Community Involvement**:
    - Engages Panchayats, schools, and community workers in **monitoring high-risk households** regularly.

5. **Breaks the Cycle of Exploitation**:
    - By identifying and addressing root causes like poverty, lack of education, or parental absence it **reduces the supply chain** for child traffickers and exploiters.

Forming of Teams

Chapter 4:
The Convergence Model

In the previous chapters, I highlighted that the first and most essential step in addressing child labour is identifying the child. Once identified, the next critical phase is assembling rescue teams equipped and prepared to carry out the rescue with care and coordination.

The morning of June 12, 2022, broke with a stillness that felt more deliberate than accidental. It was the kind of stillness that often precedes something meaningful. That day had been circled on many calendars, not just for symbolism, but for purpose. The World Day Against Child Labour.

Truth be told, I had never placed too much faith in commemorative days. Most of them passed like any other - speeches, slogans, and some media noise. But this one stayed with me. Perhaps it was the timing. I was nearing the close of my tenure with the Rajasthan State Commission for Protection of Child Rights. A time that could easily have been marked by farewells or final reports. Instead, I felt something more, a deeper urge to do something meaningful to mark the day. As I looked back on my journey, the lesson became clear : awareness by itself could not move mountains. Nor could rescue alone. We needed something sturdier. A system. A real one. Not on paper but in practice. One that could respond with speed, empathy, and coordination. No single department could achieve this. No lone NGO could shoulder the load. That is when the idea of the multi-convergence model transformed from an ideal on paper to a strategy in action. We needed everyone at the table. Not for consultation. For collaboration.

And so, we began.

With the support of the National Commission for Protection of Child Rights, we started drawing the map—departments, jurisdictions, overlaps, missing links. And slowly, we built. In Udaipur district, we formed four rescue teams. Each is assembled with care and intent: a labour officer or representative from the Labour Department, a member of the Child Welfare Committee, police from child welfare units, personnel from the Anti-Human Trafficking Unit, child protection officers, NGO partners, and field social workers.

On paper, it looked deceptively simple: Identify. Verify. Rescue. Rehabilitate.

But beneath those words were human beings each giving their time, energy, and resolve. Not for show. But for the children.

By May, the gears began to turn. Surveys were launched. Leads were followed. Every police station was given a cluster. NGO partners stepped in with insight that no official form could provide. For once, our plan did not feel rushed. It felt layered. Intentional.

We were not bracing for a one-day operation. We were building a framework to outlast any one posting, any one name.

Then came June 12. The operations began.

They continued for seven days, until June 20. And in those seven days, the model proved itself. Ninety-one children were rescued. Some were barely five years old. Some had never touched a pencil. They came from dark corners, tired, frightened and uncertain. Some were too shaken to speak. But what mattered most was, we didn't just rescue them. We had a plan for what came next.

Sixty of them re-entered school. The Education Department stood with us, supported by Article 21A of the Constitution and the Right to Education Act. The rest were placed in safe shelters through the Child Welfare Committees, with access to counselling. The work was not always flawless. Some calls went unanswered. Some files moved slower than they should have. But the structure endured. And that meant everything. Because the children were safe.

The law stood with us. Section 3A of the Child and Adolescent Labour (Prohibition and Regulation) Act talks about Prohibition of employment of adolescents in certain hazardous occupations and processes. During the week-long rescue operations, 22 FIRs were filed, resulting in the rescue of children from child labour and legal action being taken against the perpetrators.

But if I had to name the true success of that week, it would not lie in any press release. It would not rest in the numbers. It would be in the hands and hearts of those who stood together shoulder to shoulder.

It would be in the district officer who waited well past midnight to ensure a rescued child had a proper meal.

It would be in the police constable who sat beside a boy and answered every hesitant question with care.

It would be in the NGO worker who visited a family four times over, just to make sure they were truly alright.

Those acts never made headlines. But they held the model together.

To sustain this, we crafted a Standard Operating Procedure, a guide, not bound by rigidity but open to adaptation. Our NGO partners did not stop at rescue. They followed through. They stayed connected. They kept the children from slipping back into the shadows.

And through it all, I was reminded: this was never one person's mission. It never could be.

Every rescue, every recovery, every fragile success stood upon the shoulders of teams of people moved not by duty, but by conviction. People who still believe, despite setbacks, that children deserve better.

Highlights

Key Stakeholders & Their Roles in Child Labour Rescue

1. **Labour Department (Labour Officer/Inspector):**
    - *Role:* Identification and verification of child labour cases; legal action against employers.
    - Labour officers are primary in initiating and documenting child labour violations under the Child and Adolescent Labour Act.

2. **Child Welfare Committee (CWC) Members:**
   - *Role:* Ensuring immediate care and protection post-rescue; legal guardian status for rescued children.
   - CWCs are the legal authority under the Juvenile Justice Act to decide temporary and long-term rehabilitation needs.

3. **Police (Child Welfare Police Officer and Anti-Human Trafficking Unit):**
   - *Role:* Providing safety during the rescue, registering FIRs against employers, and handling any criminal violations.
   - CWPOs must accompany rescue teams and ensure legal procedures are followed. AHTUs provide intelligence and logistical support.

4. **Child Protection Unit/DCPU Officials:**
   - *Role:* Coordinating post-rescue follow-ups, linking children with counselling, education, shelter, and support schemes.
   - District Child Protection Units are mandated to develop individual care plans and oversee rehabilitation processes.

5. **NGOs and Civil Society Organizations:**
   - Assisting in identification and verification through community networks; leading on-

ground rescue coordination and rehabilitation follow-up.

6. **Education Department:**
   - Re-enrollment of rescued children in age-appropriate classes; providing support under Article 21A of the Constitution and the RTE Act.
   - Education officials are expected to ensure children are mainstreamed and supported with necessary documentation and learning assistance.

7. **District Administration (Collector/ADM/SDM):**
   - Supervisory authority for inter-departmental convergence and accountability; resource mobilization.

8. **Counsellor and Social Workers:**
   - *Role:* Providing trauma-informed care to rescued children; preparing psycho-social assessments and family reintegration support.

Highlights of the Model's Strengths:

- **Shared Ownership:** No single entity acted in isolation; each played a distinct, coordinated role in both rescue and rehabilitation.

- **Clarity of Roles:** The SOP served as a backbone for action—clearly defining who does what, when, and how.

- **Post-Rescue Continuity:** Follow-up was not treated as an afterthought. It was integrated from the beginning, with NGOs and CWCs ensuring no child slipped through the cracks.

- **Legal Framework in Action:** Provisions under the Child Labour Act and JJ Act were actively used—not just as guidelines but as instruments of justice.

Conducting Rescues

Chapter 5:
The Moving Train: Beyond the Plan

The call came like a whisper: urgent, quivering, impossible to ignore. It was a tip-off from an unnamed source, someone who chose to stay in the shadows. But I didn't need a name. I had heard this voice before too many times. That familiar tremble of alarm. Children were being trafficked again. Eight of them. This time, the route led from Mawli to Ahmedabad, towards the bangles and jewellery units, where small, tender hands are swallowed by machinery and the sparkle of childhood disappears under soot and silence.

We were told they would pass through Udaipur, either through Ranapratap Nagar or Udaipur City railway station. The margin for error? One hour.

And when a child's fate hangs by a minute, hesitation becomes a betrayal.

This incident stands in direct contradiction to what I've written in previous chapters, that before any rescue, planning is essential. And no doubt, that remains true. You must plan. You must prepare. But sometimes, the stakes are so high and the danger so immediate that there is no time to plan. You have to act. Swiftly. Decisively. Without hesitation.

I moved quickly. Alerted the railway police and RPF. Called in my team. This was not our first operation.

Sadly, far from it. But each one is never like the last. Each carries its own weight, its own urgency. Because each time, it is someone's childhood that is being snatched away.

We split into two teams. Half moved toward Udaipur City station. The others headed to Ranapratap Nagar. I chose Udaipur City. I knew it would be busier and more chaotic, with more noise to sift through.

The station was alive with motion. Trains arriving and departing. Vendors hawking tea and peanuts. Porters shouting above the din. But I wasn't distracted. But I wasn't distracted. I was looking for a different kind of presence, the presence of innocent faces of those about to be taken for labor.

You learn to recognize it: the silence of trafficked children. It is not like ordinary quiet. It is dense. It cloaks them like an invisible shroud. Still. Subdued. Too heavy for their age.

As the train pulled in, we sprang into action. With me on this rescue were Nitin Paliwal and Payal Kaneriya, both integral members of my team. The Railway Childline team was also there. We boarded the compartments, scanning row by row. Every child, every adult, every face. And then we found them.

Eight children. Huddled together. Quiet. Too quiet. Flanked by two men. The men didn't raise suspicion at first glance. They looked like regular passengers. But their posture betrayed them, hovering too closely,

At the shelter, they didn't cry. They didn't ask why. Some clung to our sleeves like they were reaching for certainty. Others just sat there, silent and unmoving, eyes fixed on the floor. It is this silence that lingers long after the operation ends.

Not the shouts at the station. Not the arrest.

It is the silence of children who have already seen too much, too soon.

Highlights

1. Railway Protection Force (RPF)

- First responder when a child is found at the station or on a train.
- Takes the child under protection and assesses their situation.
- Hands over the child to the Government Railway Police (GRP).
- Maintains detailed records of the rescued child.
- If found after 8 PM, keep the child in a safe space till the next morning.

2. Government Railway Police (GRP)

- Takes legal custody of the child from RPF.
- Produces the child before the Child Welfare Committee (CWC).
- Investigates in case of suspected trafficking or abuse.

3. RPF Inspector / Child Welfare Officer (CWO)

- Supervises all child protection activities at the station.
- Coordinates with NGOs, GRP, and CWC.
- Conducts regular meetings with stakeholders.
- Ensures production of children before the CWC.

4. Station Master / Sr. Station Manager

- Maintains the Child Assistance Booth (safe space).
- Provides emergency food, water, medical aid, and shelter.
- Keeps emergency contact numbers accessible.
- Coordinates child protection services at the station level.

5. Train Ticket Examiner (TTE)

- Identifies suspicious or unaccompanied children on trains.
- Reports cases to onboard RPF personnel.
- Assists in gathering child identity from ticket charts.

6. RPF Escort Staff (on trains)

- Monitors trains for vulnerable children.
- Assesses child safety and collects information.

- Alerts upcoming stations to prepare a rescue.
- Ensures safe handover to GRP.

7. Ticket Collector (TC)

- Identifies children in need of care and protection.
- Informs and refers the case to the RPF Inspector.

8. CHILDLINE (1098)

- Collaborate with RPF and GRP for child protection.
- Provides counselling, temporary care, and support.
- Participates in rescue and rehabilitation efforts.

9. Child Welfare Committee (CWC)

- Statutory body under the Juvenile Justice Act.
- Makes legal decisions for the care and rehabilitation of the child.
- Receives the child from GRP for further action.

10. Non-Governmental Organizations (NGOs)

- Manage or support safe spaces and shelters.
- Provide emotional support, rehabilitation, and follow-up.
- Work in coordination with RPF, GRP, and CHILDLINE.

12. Child Protection Committee (CPC)

- Formed at major railway stations.
- Oversees child safety measures and interventions.
- Coordinates between railway, police, and NGOs.
- Ensures staff training and data collection.

13. Other Supporting Stakeholders (e.g., Coolies, Vendors, Taxi/Rickshaw Drivers, Public)

- Help identify and report children in distress.
- Guide children to the RPF or Child Assistance Booth.
- Act as informants or witnesses in rescue cases.

Chapter 6:
Baal Swaraj - Beyond Borders

The events of June 12, 2022, affirmed what we had long believed possible: we had built a system that worked. The multi-convergence model, developed under the guidance of the National Commission for Protection of Child Rights (NCPCR), had successfully brought together government departments, NGOs, and the police in coordinated and purposeful action. It gave us hope. That hope had already been tested in an even larger rescue operation conducted earlier, an effort that pushed beyond state borders, strained logistical capacities, and challenged emotional boundaries. For the two states involved, it was not just a matter of coordination; it was a test of trust, urgency, and shared responsibility in protecting the most vulnerable.

It was September 29, 2019. A date I will carry with me forever. The air that day was heavy. Not with the usual weight of a rescue, but with the knowledge that this would be one of the largest interstate operations ever attempted. This was not just another case of child labour. This was a case of systematic and organized trafficking.

The lead had come from Bachpan Bachao Andolan, the organization founded by Nobel Peace Laureate Kailash Satyarthi. From the initial information, we found that approximately fifty children, mostly tribal, had been trafficked from the blocks of Gogunda, Sayra, and Kotda in Udaipur. They had been traced to the industrial Puna area in Surat, Gujarat. Lured with promises of school and better futures, they were instead found in factories, robbed of their dreams and dignity.

This was not an ordinary rescue operation. After much thought, I named it Operation Baal Swaraj. I still remember the details vividly. On December 24, 2019, I informed my then chairperson of the Rajasthan State Commission for Protection of Child Rights, Mrs. Sangeeta Beniwal, about the entire incident and the anonymous complaint. I also informed the Chief Minister's Office in Rajasthan, knowing that the holidays were approaching and interstate permissions would be difficult to secure. But the government, across various departments, trusted me. The operation received official approval on December 27, and the order was issued. I was not only asked to form a team, but also told that if anything went wrong, the entire responsibility would fall on me. If there was any failure, the operation would be presented as an effort to trace missing children from Rajasthan, not as a state-led mission.

Time was of the essence. The rescue had to begin on December 27 without any delay. I immediately reached out to the then Udaipur District Collector, who responded with great sensitivity. Mrs. Anandi (IAS) understood the urgency, and for forming the team, I chose people I knew would be ideal for a sensitive rescue like this. This included Shyam Singh Charan, the then in-charge of the Anti-Human Trafficking Unit, and Jignesh Dave, a member of the Child Welfare Committee. Alongside them were Dhananjay Tingal, the senior representative of BBA; Manish Sharma, a child labour rescue expert and then police staff Bhanu Pratap Singh Solanki, among others. Vehicles were arranged—two buses and two taxis—carefully selected to avoid creating the impression of a government operation. The goal was to keep the traffickers unaware of our entry into Gujarat.

What followed was true convergence in its most demanding form. The Rajasthan State Commission for Protection of Child Rights activated every possible resource: Anti-Human Trafficking Units, Child Welfare Committees, District Child Protection Units, and reliable NGO partners. Simultaneously, Gujarat police began mobilising their network. Two states and two governments, with multiple departments, shared one common goal.

Preparation was vital. We mapped factory locations, identified holding areas, and traced transportation patterns used by traffickers. Weeks of silent reconnaissance followed. Every detail was cross-checked. Every risk assessed. Our teams worked quietly, gathering intelligence and bracing themselves for what we knew would be an enormous, emotionally charged task.

On the ground, NGOs were our backbone. Their local knowledge was invaluable. They were not just our eyes and ears. They were also the first to reach the children. Without them, we would have been lost in the maze of hidden workshops and tight alleyways.

The Gujarat police were informed the night before. We told them that some of our missing children were believed to be in the state and we would be conducting an operation. We needed their support.

At dawn on December 29, while Surat still slept, we moved.

In a carefully coordinated strike, multiple teams stormed targeted sites at the same time. Some doors resisted. Others swung open. And behind those doors, we saw it. Children some no older than seven working in silence. Their faces were blank. Their backs bent. They froze when they saw us. Some ran. Some tried to hide. Two boys were found in a cupboard. Others were curled up on thin, torn blankets. Many of them didn't even remember how long they had been there.

Each team had a task. One secured the premises. Another identified children. Some teams handled documentation, while others ensured immediate care and arranged transport. The model worked like a symphony. Every team is in sync. Every movement is purposeful.

And what we discovered confirmed our worst fears.

The traffickers had violated several laws. The Child and Adolescent Labour (Prohibition and Regulation) Act of 1986 had been breached. Section 370 of the Indian Penal Code, which addresses trafficking, was invoked. Sections 75 and 79 of the Juvenile Justice Act, covering cruelty and bonded labour, applied too. The Factories Act was relevant as well, because these weren't factories, they were cages.

When the operation began that morning, I had expected around fifty children. But as we moved through one locked room after another, the numbers grew. One locked room had thick smoke coming from inside, triggering panic. We feared the worst, a sudden blaze in the middle of an already tense operation. But as we forced the door open, the truth became stranger than we expected: it was the children cooking food inside a room without any ventilation. They could not eat once their shift began. We couldn't stand there for five minutes. These children had been living in that smoke for years.

In just a few hours, we had rescued eighty children. Some were hidden under bundles of sarees in factory storerooms. But our alert officers located them all. When the number crossed one hundred, I informed the Chief Minister and the Commission in Rajasthan. The entire state was shaken by the scale of this tragedy.

Suddenly, this operation became more than a rescue. It became a statewide moment of reckoning. The Hon'ble Chief Minister and the Chairperson of RSCPCR called me personally, checking in and wishing us a safe return. Soon after, the national and international media took note. This had become a story the entire country was talking about.

But we were not finished. Our priority was ensuring the safety of these children. As the media buzzed, my focus remained on transport and security. We had filed a zero FIR in Rajasthan before we left, and with the help of Gujarat authorities, a large police force was deployed to protect us. This turned out to be crucial soon after the rescue, a large mob attempted to free the children. They tried to attack our group. But thanks to swift support from both state governments, we avoided a disaster.

Once the children were out of danger, we began hearing their stories. They spoke to us. They cried. They whispered the truths they had kept hidden. And they thanked us.

FIRs were filed. Factory owners and middlemen were identified. Evidence was collected and processed.

But our duty did not end there.

The children were placed under the protection of Child Welfare Committees. Medical checkups were conducted. Psychological support was offered. Some children had visible injuries. Others had invisible scars.

Many children had no documents. Our teams worked with the District Child Protection Units to trace their families. Some children were reunited. Others were given safe homes in long-term care facilities.

Rehabilitation was not just a process. It was a promise.

Our NGO partners stayed the course. They conducted follow-ups, verified family claims, and ensured every child had support.

Every stakeholder did their part:

➢ The police ensured protection and filed legal cases.

➢ Childline and NGOs offered comfort and continuity.

➢ The Labour Department investigated workplace violations.

➢ Education and Social Welfare brought children back to school.

➢ Legal teams pursued justice in court.

➢ CWCs and DCPUs made recovery plans and watched closely so no child was forgotten.

More charges followed under the Bonded Labour Abolition Act, the Factories Act, and Section 374 of the IPC, which prohibits forced labour.

That return journey changed everything.

I remember the bus. I remember the silence at first. The children stared out at the road. They whispered. They waited.

And then, a sound.

One child clapped.

Another began to sing.

Soon, the bus was filled with laughter and songs. Children sang folk tunes. They banged tambourines made of hands and bus seats. They danced. They laughed. They celebrated. It was unfiltered. Raw. Beautiful.

That bus ride was more than a journey back home.

It was freedom reclaimed.

Looking back, this operation was not only about rescuing one hundred and thirty-eight children. It was about reaffirming something much deeper. It reminded us, and the world, that every child deserves freedom. Their happiness is not a privilege. It is their birthright.

We didn't just rescue children.

We reignited one hundred and thirty-eight flames of hope.

Satisfying Experience

1. That rescue on December 29, 2019, was never meant to be a one-time effort. It became the foundation of the strongest network I have built to date, a network shaped by courageous officers, alert citizens, and a few committed members of the media who stood by us during that operation and have remained part of my circle ever since.

2. Even now I continue to receive calls, especially when a child from Rajasthan is discovered in child labour or found in distress, far from home.

3. As I sit writing this book on April 17, 2025, another such moment arrived. Around 10 p.m., a call came in. Four children from Jhadol Panchayat in Udaipur district had been found in Surat, identified by a local resident who did not just stop at reporting. He helped ensure their rescue, filed an FIR at the Puna Police Station in Surat, and assisted in the arrest of two individuals involved. The children were safely brought back to Udaipur.

Chapter 7:
Bonded Childhood

It was 24 July 2024. The kind of evening that should pass uneventfully. I had just finished noting down updates from an earlier visit, preparing to leave for the day, when the phone rang. The voice on the other end belonged to a local volunteer. Calm, but concerned.

A child had been found near a restaurant in the Kotwali area of Chittorgarh district, Rajasthan. A boy. Alone. Curled up on the pavement. No belongings. Too tired to speak. Too wary to ask for help. These calls are not new. But they are never ordinary.

I wasn't in Chittorgarh at the time, I was about 150 kilometers away, in Udaipur. I couldn't reach the child immediately.

That's when my team stepped in. Amit Rao, our district coordinator for Chittorgarh, was informed and rushed to the location. He found the boy huddled under a thin, torn blanket, lying on the ground as though it were the only place left in the world for him. His clothes were soiled, his face hollow. Amit sat beside him and gently asked if he was okay. The boy didn't answer right away. His eyes studied Amit's. But slowly, he reached for the blanket offered. Took a sip of water.

His name was Chirag. (name changed)

He said he was ten years old, from Ratlam in Madhya Pradesh. And then, piece by piece, his story began to unfold.

About a year ago, his uncle had taken him to Rampuriya, a small village tucked into Rajasthan. There, in an act far too common and far too cruel, Chirag was handed over to a family in exchange for ₹36,000. They needed help with household chores, and the money was the price of his freedom.

From that day forward, Chirag became their full-time worker.

He herded goats. He swept the courtyards. He cleaned animal waste. He washed dishes. His day began before the first light touched the village and ended long after the household went to sleep. Any mistake, any delay, was met with blows.

This was not just child labour. It was something more sinister. More structured. This was bonded labour, a form of servitude where a child's life becomes currency. Where work replaces play. Where pain replaces protection.

The ₹36,000 wasn't just a payment. It was an invisible shackle—a contract that no one wrote down, but everyone enforced. Chirag was expected to "repay" the sum through his body, through his silence, and through his stolen years.

"I want to go home. I want to study," he whispered. That whisper was a cry for justice.

He had studied up to the third grade. Since then, he had only watched from a distance as other children made their way to school. He watched them laugh, run, and carry books. He carried firewood.

My team, along with the child helpline team, took the child to the District Child Welfare Committee. His identity was confirmed. His situation was verified. He was placed in a shelter, given care, and recognized rightfully as a child trapped in bonded labour. This is more common than many would like to believe, especially in rural corners where desperation and debt often pave the path to exploitation.

As my team spent more time with him, the full truth emerged that Chirag had escaped on his own.

One night, while the family slept, he found a bicycle. With no clear sense of direction, only the fire of determination, he pedalled toward Ratlam. He rode for hours, the night sky his only witness. Until exhaustion overcame him. He collapsed near the restaurant where he was found.

The next steps were clear. We had to trace his family. Prepare him for return. Ensure that his case was formally documented. Though the family who had kept him and the uncle who sold him were not yet traceable, we shifted our focus to something more urgent: his recovery.

Since the case was of bonded labour, the children have to be presented before the SDM of the concerned area and the release certificate has to be issued. After the efforts of senior advocate of IJM John James who assisted in this work and made the SDM aware of the entire process, the RC was issued and the child was freed from bonded labour with a freedom certificate.

Eventually, Chirag was reunited with his parents. Regular telephonic follow-up was done and the child and his parents enrolled him back into the school. Government support schemes were linked to the family to ease their economic burden. These may seem like small steps, but in the life of a child, they are transformative.

Because this was never just about a boy working in a home.

This was about a system that allowed a child to be bartered. It was about a society that had normalized the idea that a boy could be "taken," "used," and "kept" in exchange for money. It was about a silent agreement written not on paper, but into our apathy that some children are worth less than others.

Even within the cruelest systems, hope survives. But hope alone will never be enough. We must act. Bonded labour is not merely about work; it is about control. It is about silence. It is about the theft of freedom.

And no child, no matter where they are born should ever have to live like that.

After Chirag's case, I spent some time thinking not just about his journey, but also about the system that allowed such a thing to happen in the first place.

He was a child, made to work day and night, far away from home, with no pay and no schooling. For most people, that would immediately qualify as child labour. And they would be right. But there was more to it. His story also pointed to a deeper, more concealed form of exploitation—bonded labour.

How Are Bonded Labour and Child Labour Connected?

The two are closely linked. **Child labour** refers to any work that deprives children of their childhood, education, and development. It includes children working on farms, in factories, in shops, homes, or on the streets. Not all child labour is bonded labour, but many cases of bonded labour involve children.

Bonded child labour is when a child is forced to work because of a debt, an advance taken by a family member, or a social obligation. Often, these children are unable to leave the work, are underpaid or not paid at all, and are made to work under the threat of punishment or violence.

In Chirag's case, his uncle accepted money in exchange for placing him in a household. Chirag did not choose to work there. He had no say in how long he would work, when he would return, or what kind of life he would live. His labour became a way to "repay" a transaction he had no role in. That made it bonded labour, and because he was underage, it was bonded child labour.

Where Does This Happen?

It happens in many places:

- In villages, where children herd cattle or work in brick kilns.
- In homes, where they work as domestic help.
- In roadside stalls, workshops, or factories.
- In agriculture and small businesses.

In many cases, children do not even realise they are working under bondage. They are told to work for the family's sake, to "help out," or to "repay" someone's kindness. This normalisation makes it even harder to detect and report.

How Can It Be Identified?

Bonded labour especially when it involves children can often be identified by:

- Long working hours with no rest.
- Little or no wages.
- An advance or lump-sum paid to the family or relative.
- Restrictions on movement or communication.
- No access to education.

- Threats, abuse, or punishment if the child tries to leave.

The presence of any of these signs should be taken seriously. These are not just poor work conditions. They are signs of exploitation.

Elements of Bonded Labour

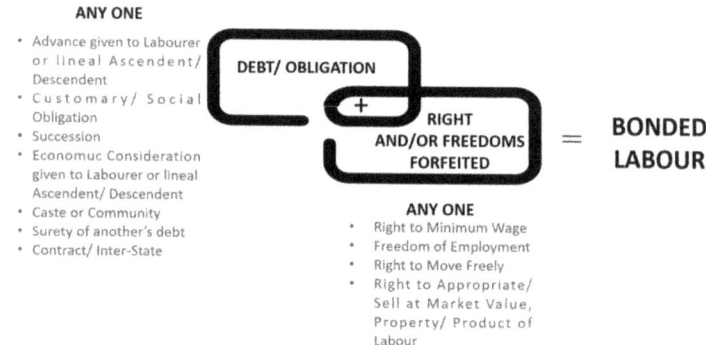

Where Can You Report It?

If bonded child labour is suspected, a complaint can be made at:

- The **nearest Police Station**.
- **The Collector and District Magistrate's office**.
- The **Labour Department**
- Child protection services or helplines like **Childline (1098)**.

Local NGOs and Child Rights Organisations often help in coordinating rescue, legal support, and rehabilitation.

What Happens After Rescue?

Once a child is rescued from bonded labour, several steps follow:

1. **Immediate support** is provided like food, shelter, medical care, and psychological support.
2. The **District Administration** conducts an inquiry.
3. If confirmed, a **Release Certificate** is issued.
4. The child is linked with **rehabilitation schemes**, including:
    - Financial compensation
    - Enrolment in school
    - Housing or land assistance (if eligible)
    - Skill development (for older children or family members)
    - Linkages to welfare schemes like ration, health cards, and job support

One important point to remember is that **financial assistance does not depend on punishment of the offender**. The child's rehabilitation starts right away, which helps prevent further harm or delay.

Why Does This Continue to Happen?

Despite clear protections, bonded child labour still continues due to:

- Poverty and lack of awareness in families.
- Pressure to earn from a young age.
- Weak law enforcement at the local level.
- Deep-rooted social structures and informal systems of labour.
- Gaps in access to education and social safety nets.

In areas where poverty is high and schooling is limited, children are most at risk of being pulled into work early—and often into conditions that qualify as bonded labour.

Children like Chirag remind us that child labour is not always out in the open. Sometimes it hides behind words like "help," "obligation," or "custom." It can be inside someone's house, on a farm, or far away in another state. Often, it is tied to the practice of bonded labour—where a child's work becomes a form of repayment, and their freedom is quietly taken away.

We cannot talk about child labour without addressing the hidden, complex system of bondage that continues to trap children. And we cannot end bonded labour without recognising how many of its victims are children, whose lives are being shaped by circumstances they never chose.

Our responsibility is not just to rescue. It is to restore. And most importantly, to prevent.

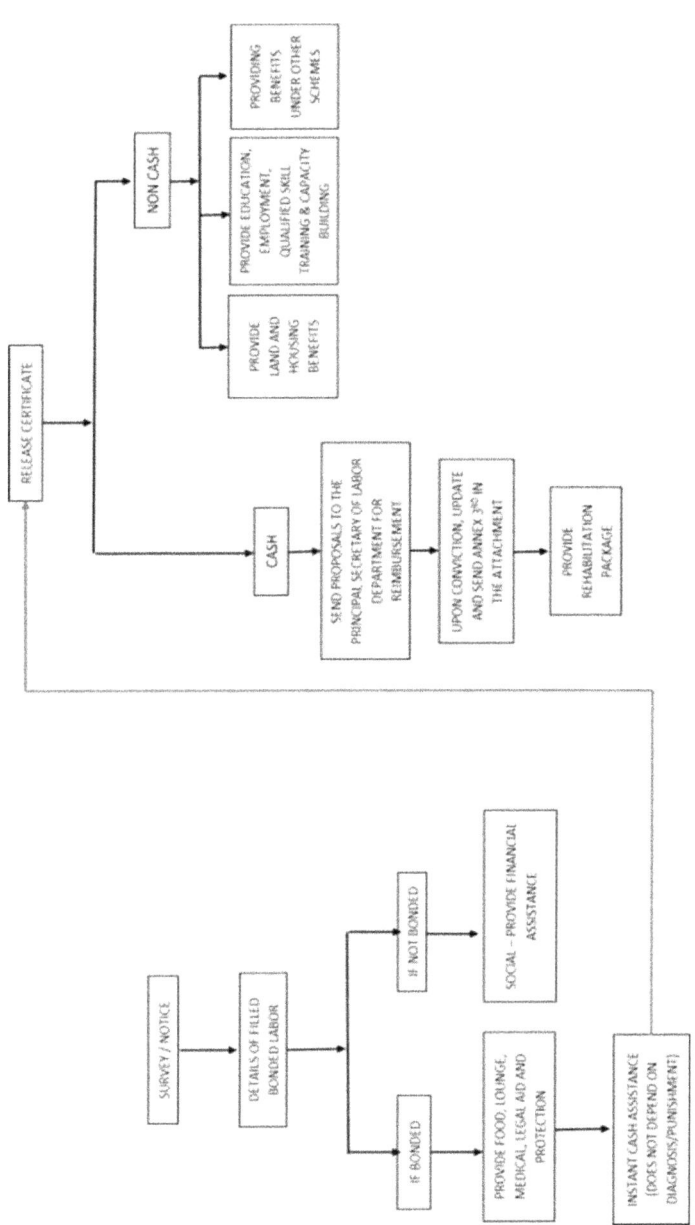

Registering First Information Report (FIR)

Chapter 08:
Model FIR

On hearing the words Model FIR, a question immediately arises: what exactly is a "Model FIR"? But before that, what is meant by a model case?

"Model FIR (First Information Report) are FIRs that are not registered based on a single act, such as the Child Labour Abolition Act, but rather are designed to cover all possible forms of child exploitation. The goal is simply to ensure that the victim receives maximum justice and the culprit faces the harshest punishment possible."

To achieve this, it becomes absolutely necessary that the rescuer, the person who first comes to the aid of the victim, fully understand the circumstances of the rescue. They must see through the lens of various laws and thoughtfully connect the victim's situation to all relevant legal sections.

For example, look at the photograph below. It captures the aftermath of a child labour rescue operation. Notice how many different legal sections have been invoked, each one playing a role in strengthening the case.

I.I.F.-I /एकीकृत जाप 1

FIRST INFORMATION REPORT
(Under Section 154 Cr.P.C.)
(प्रथम सूचना रिपोर्ट)
(धारा 154 दण्ड प्रक्रिया संहिता के तहत)

1. District   P.S.   Year
   (जिला):   (थाना):   (वर्ष):

2. FIR No.   Date and Time of FIR
   (प्र.सू.रि.सं): (एफआईआर की तिथि/समय):   3 00:11 बजे

S.No. (क्र.सं.)	Acts (अधिनियम)	Sections (धाराएँ)
1	भा दं सं 1860	370(5)
2	भा दं सं 1860	344
3	भा दं सं 1860	374
4	किशोर न्याय (बच्चों की देखभाल और संरक्षण) अधिनियम 2015	75
5	किशोर न्याय (बच्चों की देखभाल और संरक्षण) अधिनियम 2015	79
6	बालक श्रम (प्रतिषेध और विनियमन) अधिनियम, 1986	3
7	बालक श्रम (प्रतिषेध और विनियमन) अधिनियम, 1986	14
8	बंधित श्रम पद्धति (उन्मूलन) अधिनियम, 1976	16
9	बंधित श्रम पद्धति (उन्मूलन) अधिनियम, 1976	17
10	बंधित श्रम पद्धति (उन्मूलन) अधिनियम, 1976	18

3. (a) Occurrence of offence (अपराध की घटना):

   1. Day(दिन):   Date From   Date To
                     (दिनांक से):   (दिनांक तक):

   Time Period   Time From   Time To
   (समय अवधि)   (समय से):   (समय तक):

This chapter serves as a reference guide for filing First Information Reports (FIRs) in cases involving trafficking, child Labour, bonded Labour, and child exploitation. It outlines relevant legal provisions under various Acts to ensure that all applicable charges are invoked during FIR registration. This approach strengthens prosecution and rehabilitation outcomes for survivors.

A. The Bharatiya Nyaya Sanhita (BNS), 2024

Section	Explanation
Section 143 (2)	Trafficking in person.
Section 143 (3)	Trafficking of more than one person.
Section 143 (4)	Trafficking of Child.
Section 143 (5)	Trafficking of more than one child.
Section 143 (6)	Trafficking in person.
Section 143 (7)	Public servant or police officer involved in trafficking of persons.
Section 144	Exploitation of trafficked person.
Section 111	Organized Crime.
Section 145	Habitual dealing in slaves.
Section 146	Unlawful compulsory labour.
Section 115 (1)	Voluntary causing hurt.
Section 115 (2)	Voluntary causing grievous hurt.
Section 126 (2)	Wrongful Restraint.
Section 127 (1)	Wrongful Confinement.
Section 140 (4)	Kidnapping or abducting to subject person to slavery.
Section 142	Wrongfully concealing or keeping confined a kidnapped or abducted person.
Section 351 (2)	Criminal intimidation
Section 351 (3)	Criminal intimidation by threat to cause death or grievous hurt.
Section 318 (2)	Cheating

B. Child and Adolescent Labour (Prohibition and Regulation) Act, 1986 (amended 2016)

Section	Explanation
Section 3,14(1)	Employing or allowing a child to work in any job or process, except for non-hazardous family businesses or safe audio-visual entertainment, is permitted only if the child continues their education.
Section 3A, 14 (1A)	Employing or allowing any adolescent to work in hazardous occupation or processes listed in the CLA schedule is prohibited.
Section 14	Contravention of any other provision under CLA.

C. Bonded Labour System (Abolition) Act, 1976

Section	Explanation
Section 9 (2)	Whoever accepts any payment from a labourer against a bonded debt.
Section 16	Whoever compels any person to provide bonded labour.
Section 17	Whoever advances a bonded debt.
Section 18	Whoever enforces any custom, tradition, contract or agreement requiring a person to work under a bonded labour system.
Section 19	Whoever omits or fails to restore any property of a bonded labour.

D. Juvenile Justice (Care and Protection of Children) Act, 2015

Section	Explanation
Section 75	Punishment for cruelty to Child.

Section 76 (1)	Employs child for begging of causing child to beg.
Section 79	Engaging and keeping child in bondage for the purpose of employment or withholding earnings or using earnings for own purpose.
Section 81	Buying and selling of children for any purpose

E. SC/ST (Prevention of Atrocities) Act of 1989

Section	Explanation
Section 3 (1) h	Making a SC/ST member to do beggar or any other form of bonded labour.
Section 3 (2) (v)	Commits an offense under BNS Punishable with 10 years or more against a member of SC/ST

F. Inter-State Migrant Workmen Act, 1979

Section	Explanation
Section 25	Contravention of provisions regarding employment or license under ISMW
Section 26	Contravention of other provisions under ISMW not punishable elsewhere

G. The Payment of Wages Act, 1936

Section	Explanation
Section 20	Penalty of Offenses under the Act

H. The Minimum Wages Act, 1948

Section	Explanation
Section 22	If employer pays to any employee less than the minimum rates of wages or contravenes any rule or order made under section 13 of the Act.

I. Protection of Children from Sexual Offence (POCSO) Act, 2012

Section	Explanation
Section 7 & 8	Sexual assault.
Section 9 & 10	Aggravated sexual assault

Medical, Age Determination, Counseling & Shelter

Chapter 09: Age Matters

During my time as a member of the State Commission there was a routine that had become strangely familiar. Every time we sought progress reports from districts on rescued children, particularly from child labour hotspots we would receive remarkably high numbers. Some districts claimed 50 rescues, some even more.

At first glance, it seemed promising. Encouraging, even.

But then we would ask the next question: *How many FIRs were filed?*

The numbers would drop drastically.

Then we asked: *How many children were presented before the Child Welfare Committee? How many were provided shelter? How many received counselling?*

The silence that followed those questions was the loudest truth of all.

A common reply from many district officers was disturbingly uniform: *"He looked like an adult, so we let him go."*

This one sentence reflected a widespread and dangerous myth that the age of a child can be judged by appearance alone. As if childhood could be measured by height, facial hair, or tone of voice. This myth is not only scientifically flawed but it is legally impermissible.

Under Section 94 of the Juvenile Justice (Care and Protection of Children) Act the procedure for age determination is clearly defined:

(1) Where, it is obvious to the Committee or the Board, based on the appearance of the person brought before it under any of the provisions of this Act (other than for the purpose of giving evidence) that the said person is a child, the Committee or the Board shall record such observation stating the age of the child as nearly as may be and proceed with the inquiry under section 14 or section 36, as the case may be, without waiting for further confirmation of the age.

(2) In case, the Committee or the Board has reasonable grounds for doubt regarding whether the person brought before it is a child or not, the Committee or the Board, as the case may be, shall undertake the process of age determination, by seeking evidence by obtaining—

(i) the date of birth certificate from the school, or the matriculation or equivalent certificate from the concerned examination Board, if available; and in the absence thereof;

(ii) the birth certificate given by a corporation or a municipal authority or a panchayat;

(iii) and only in the absence of (i) and (ii) above, age shall be determined by an ossification test or any other latest medical age determination test conducted on the orders of the Committee or the Board:

Provided such an age determination test conducted on the order of the Committee or the Board shall be completed within fifteen days from the date of such order.

(3) The age recorded by the Committee or the Board to be the age of the person so brought before it shall, for the purpose of this Act, be deemed to be the true age of that person.

Nowhere in this legal provision does it say a police officer, or even a well-meaning rescuer, can decide the age based on personal judgment. That power lies exclusively with the Child Welfare Committee (CWC), the only competent authority to make such a determination.

But herein lies the problem. In the absence of proper medical examination and legal procedure, children are freed prematurely. In fact, many are sent back to the same cycle of abuse they were rescued from. No rehabilitation. No justice.

This is where the role of medical checks becomes not just necessary, but urgent. Medical teams are not only responsible for age determination through ossification and other tests, but they are often the first to discover injuries, visible and invisible. Signs of physical trauma. Undernourishment. In some cases, even sexual abuse. A rescue without medical intervention is incomplete and careless.

Equally critical is counselling. A child who has been trafficked, exploited, or enslaved cannot simply "move on" after being rescued. Their trauma does not end at the police station. It begins to surface in the quiet moments when they lie awake at night in an unfamiliar bed, unsure of who to trust.

The Protection of Children from Sexual Offences (POCSO) Act, 2012 and the Juvenile Justice Act, 2015 both emphasize the need for psychosocial support. Counselling is not an option, it is a mandate. Social workers and counsellors must be part of every rescue and follow-up.

And then comes shelter, perhaps the most underrated but most essential part of the recovery process. A child cannot heal on the street or at a police station. They need safety, warmth, and routine. This is why, under the Juvenile Justice Act, the Child Welfare Committee must immediately place the child in a registered Child Care Institution (CCI) or another safe space pending further inquiry.

Shelter homes are not simply buildings. They are safe places. Places where a child can breathe again. Think again. Dream again.

In one district, when we followed up on a report of 28 rescued children, we found that only nine had been formally presented before the CWC. When questioned, the officer said, *"They looked big. They didn't look like children."*

This visual misjudgment denies the child their constitutional right to protection, and more critically, their right to justice.

As per Juvenile Justice Act, the CWC is the final authority in matters of child protection, including age verification and shelter recommendations. The law is unambiguous.

> "The Committee shall have the authority to deal exclusively with all proceedings under this Act, relating to children in need of care and protection."

This includes issuing orders for medical examination, assigning social workers, ensuring legal aid, and directing placement in a shelter.

To ignore this process is to fail the child all over again.

In every rescue, the chain of protection must begin the moment a child is recovered. It must move from rescue → medical → counselling → CWC → shelter → rehabilitation. Every missing link is a missed opportunity. Every shortcut is a scope to a new crime.

If the rescue is the first step, the restoration of dignity is the destination.

And it is not only about one child. It is about the message we send to thousands more waiting in factories, fields, homes, and brothels. Children whose ages have been miscalculated and whose innocence has been disregarded.

A system that merely rescues, but does not rehabilitate, is no better than the one that exploited them in the first place.

Let us remember—age is not about how old a child looks. It is about how young they were made to suffer.

<u>Highlights</u>

Legally, the power to determine the age of a child does not rest with police or any administrative officer. That authority is exclusively vested in the Child Welfare Committee under the Juvenile Justice (Care and Protection of Children) Act, 2015.

Relevant Legal Provisions:

- Section 94 of the Juvenile Justice (Care and Protection of Children) Act, 2015

Under Section 94 of the Juvenile Justice (Care and Protection of Children) Act the procedure for age determination is clearly defined:

(1) Where, it is obvious to the Committee or the Board, based on the appearance of the person brought before it under any of the provisions of this Act (other than for the purpose of giving evidence) that the said person is a child, the Committee or the Board shall record such observation stating the age of the child as nearly as may be and proceed with the inquiry under section 14 or section 36, as the case may be, without waiting for further confirmation of the age.

(2) In case, the Committee or the Board has reasonable grounds for doubt regarding whether the person brought before it is a child or not, the Committee or the Board, as the case may be, shall undertake the process of age determination, by seeking evidence by obtaining—

(i) the date of birth certificate from the school, or the matriculation or equivalent certificate from the concerned examination Board, if available; and in the absence thereof;

(ii) the birth certificate given by a corporation or a municipal authority or a panchayat;

(iii) and only in the absence of (i) and (ii) above, age shall be determined by an ossification test or any other latest medical age determination test conducted on the orders of the Committee or the Board:

Provided such an age determination test conducted on the order of the Committee or the Board shall be completed within fifteen days from the date of such order.

(3) The age recorded by the Committee or the Board to be the age of the person so brought before it shall, for the purpose of this Act, be deemed to be the true age of that person.

- Section 36(3) of the JJ Act, 2015 mandates:

    "Where the Committee is satisfied... that the child is in need of care and protection, it may, after making due inquiry, pass appropriate orders for the care, protection, rehabilitation or restoration of the child."

These provisions clearly establish that only the CWC has the legal power to decide on the age, custody, medical examination, counselling, and rehabilitation of a rescued child.

Medical professionals are required not only to assist with age verification but also to identify signs of physical or sexual abuse. Social workers and counsellors play a critical role in providing emotional support, and CWCs are responsible for ensuring the child is placed in a Child Care Institution (CCI) or other safe accommodation.

Failure to follow this legal process often results in children being released prematurely and left vulnerable once again to trafficking, labour, and abuse.

This chapter makes it unequivocally clear: rescue is not enough. Unless we follow through with legal and protective mechanisms, including age determination, FIRs, counselling, and shelter, we are simply sending the child from one form of exploitation to another.

Rehabilitation

Chapter 10:
Rescue is Only the beginning

The joy of rescuing a child from forced labour is often short-lived. Relief is temporary. Anyone who has worked on the ground knows this simple truth: rescue is just the first step. Rehabilitation is the real journey. And it is a long one.

I remember when six children were rescued from different parts of Udaipur district, stone quarries, roadside dhabas, and construction sites. Their hands were bruised. Their bodies hunched from years of lifting, breaking, serving. Some had scars that ran along their backs. Others carried wounds no medical report could see. What we rescued them from was only half the story. The real struggle was ensuring they never went back.

What followed was a fight, not against the traffickers this time, but against the indifference of a system that often sees rescue as an endpoint.

Rescue = Immediate Relief

Rehabilitation = lasting Change

Rescue without rehabilitation is like pulling a patient out of danger but leaving them without treatment, only for them to fall back into risk. Few people understand what true rehabilitation means. Some think it is about linking children to a government scheme or offering financial help, but my experience has taught me otherwise. True rehabilitation is not only about money. It is about connecting the child to the psychological, social, and economic mainstream. Only then can we call it real rehabilitation.

Why is Rehabilitation Essential?

Restoring Rights and Dignity: Every child deserves freedom, not just from labour, but from the shame and fear it breeds.

Healing Physical and Emotional Harm: Labour leaves scars, some seen, many invisible. Rehabilitation must heal both.

Breaking the Cycle of Child Labour: Without support, rescued children often fall right back into the same exploitative conditions.

Preventing Re-trafficking and Abuse: A vulnerable child without a support system is easy prey for traffickers.

Strengthening Families and Communities: Economic insecurity often forces families into sending children to work. Strengthening them is key to real change.

Once we began following the correct legal process, a new path unfolded, one where children were not just rescued, but truly given a second chance at life. And that chance rests on three pillars of rehabilitation: social, psychological, and financial.

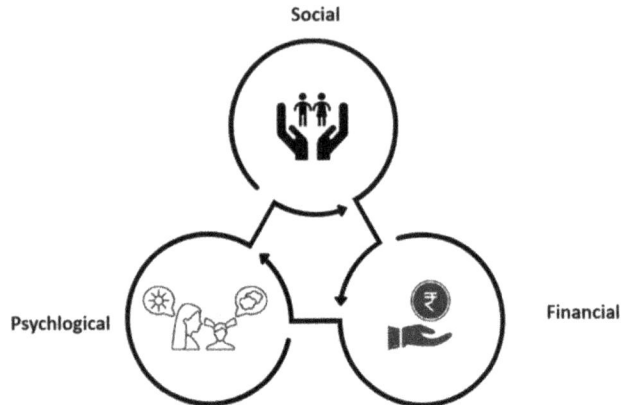

Psychological Rehabilitation: Healing the Inside First

When Mohan (name changed) was rescued from a roadside eatery, he was barely ten years old. He had worked there for over two years. Whenever someone raised their hand, even just to wave, he flinched. If asked a question, he would reply with "Sorry, I will do better." He did not know what safety looked like. He only knew how to obey.

Psychological rehabilitation is more than just counselling sessions. It is about reminding children that they are human. That they can laugh, cry, rest, without owing anyone an apology. Every child's case is different; there can be no one-size-fits-all solution. Proper counselling, ideally with help from Childline services or local NGOs, is essential. In many cases, children are taken back by their families within days of rescue. That is why families, too, must be trained on how to behave with children, how to rebuild trust, and how to nurture their healing.

Social Rehabilitation: Returning to the World

Lali and her siblings, rescued from near trafficking, had known nothing but abandonment. After their trauma was addressed, the next step was reintegration.

We enrolled them in school.

I still remember Ramesh and Suresh standing outside the school gate, nervously adjusting the straps on their brand-new backpacks.

"Will they know I cannot read?" Ramesh whispered.

"That is why you are going," I said. "To learn. Everyone starts somewhere."

Through bridge courses, peer mentoring, NGO support, and conversations with school staff, the children slowly found their rhythm. Their families were not blamed but supported, ration cards applied for, and government schemes explained.

Social rehabilitation is not just about putting a child back into school. It is about restoring their place in society with dignity.

Financial Rehabilitation: Justice in Cash

There is no greater irony than rescuing a child from labour only to send them back into poverty. Many families do not send children to work out of cruelty, but out of desperation. Without financial security, the cycle repeats.

That is why compensation matters.

One of the most powerful moments during my tenure was when many rescued children in the Udaipur division received compensation through the District Legal Services Authority (DLSA). It was not just money. It was an official acknowledgment that the state owed them justice, that what happened to them was not merely unfortunate, but unlawful.

These funds helped families buy essentials, pay school fees, and cover shelter expenses, ensuring that children no longer had to choose between hunger and freedom.

Beyond compensation, there are many social security schemes that states offer. In Rajasthan, the Palanhar Yojana is one such critical initiative. Thousands of children have been connected to it, offering them sustained support. Similarly, landmark judgments like MC Mehta provide important frameworks for ensuring state accountability.

It is easier to count rescues. Harder to count dignity. Easier to build a case file. Harder to rebuild a childhood. Every child rescued deserves not just relief, but restoration.

That is why we must stop treating rescue as a headline and start treating rehabilitation as the real story.

The road back to childhood is long. But it is a road worth walking, if we walk it together.

<u>Highlights</u>

- Social Rehabilitation: Involves school enrolment, peer integration, community acceptance, and family support through welfare schemes to ensure children are not forced back into labour.

- Psychological Rehabilitation: Focuses on emotional healing, building trust, and helping children reclaim their right to feel safe, express emotions, and recover from trauma through counselling and care.

- Financial Rehabilitation: Stresses the importance of compensation through bodies like the Legal Services Authority, Labour Department, and other state schemes as a form of restorative justice and economic support.

The chapter argues that unless these three pillars are addressed with commitment and consistency, the child remains vulnerable. True rehabilitation is not just a matter of policy, it is a matter of practice. It is about restoring dignity, not just freedom. And it only begins after the rescue.

Follow Up

Chapter 11:
The Final Step

By the time you reach this chapter, you might feel the journey is complete.

Vulnerability mapping? Done.

Identification and verification? Done.

Formation of rescue teams and community groups? Done.

Rescue operations, shelter placement, medical aid, and counselling? All checked.

FIRs lodged, compensation filed and even received.

Rehabilitation—emotional, social, psychological? Initiated and ongoing.

So, what more could be left?

One critical thing: follow-up.

This is where most systems falter not because of repulsion, but because of fatigue. There's an illusion of closure once the formal steps are complete. But we've learned the hard way: rescue without follow-up is like planting a seed and forgetting to water it. If we don't return, check in, support, and walk with the child beyond the rescue the entire chain of intervention can collapse.

And worse, the child might quietly slip back into the same trap we worked so hard to pull them out of.

Why Follow-Up Matters

Follow-up isn't a formality. It's a lifeline.

Without regular follow-up: A child might drop out of school quietly after a few weeks.

Economic pressures might force families to send them back to work.

The trauma they carry might go unaddressed, slowly eating away at their progress.

Worse still, they may become even more vulnerable, ashamed or afraid to reach out when things begin to unravel.

This is why we insist on building a follow-up mechanism that is consistent, sensitive, and time-bound. In our model, every child is followed up with for a minimum of six months, and often beyond depending on the nature of the case. It's not just paperwork. It's sitting with them under a tree after school. It's calling their teachers. It's checking on their health. It's listening, observing, and intervening when necessary.

Let me tell you about a boy we rescued from Gogunda during one of our routine child labour raids. He was thin, quiet, withdrawn, the kind of child who never speaks unless spoken to.

He had been working in a roadside dhaba, away from his family, disconnected from everything that should define childhood. We placed him in a shelter, provided counselling, and enrolled him in school. On paper, the process was complete.

But we didn't stop there.

In the months that followed, my team visited him regularly, sometimes to check on school progress, sometimes just to sit beside him during lunch, letting him know we were still there. At first, he was hesitant. He would smile politely, answer questions in monosyllables, and keep his distance.

But something shifts when a child realizes you're not going to disappear.

On our fourth visit, something changed. He lingered after our conversation. Looked over his shoulder. Then quietly said, "Can I tell you something?"

What he shared next stunned us. One of his friends, another boy from his village was being forced into child marriage. The boy was barely 14. The marriage was planned for the coming month.

Because of the trust we had built, this child had become a whistleblower. He had gone from victim to protector. We intervened swiftly, reached out to the Panchayat, halted the marriage, and ensured the boy was safe. That day, the rescued child from Gogunda reminded us:

when we follow up, we don't just protect the rescued—we unlock a ripple effect of protection.

Systemic Follow-Up: Structured, Not Sporadic

So how do we build follow-up into the system?

Set a time-bound plan: Every rescued child must be followed up for at least six months, with monthly visits or check-ins documented and actioned.

Build a multidisciplinary team: Teachers, Anganwadi workers, ASHA staff, Childline volunteers, and NGOs must coordinate. No one person can do it all.

Involve the child in their own journey: Let them set small goals, academic, personal, emotional. Celebrate their wins. Let them lead, even a little.

Check in with the school: Attendance is not the only marker. Is the child engaged? Are they making friends? Are they facing bullying or isolation?

Stay alert to signs of relapse: Sudden silence, irritability, absenteeism, or emotional withdrawal, these are not just mood swings. They often are a cry for help.

Document, document, document: Because what gets documented, gets tracked and what gets tracked, gets done.

Follow-Up is Prevention

Every child we follow up with is a story we refuse to let end in tragedy.

Every return visit is a reminder that their safety is not temporary.

Every question we ask is a message: We still see you. We still care.

Most importantly, follow-up prevents re-trafficking, re-exploitation, and re-traumatization. It converts rescue into recovery. It transforms legal aid into lived safety. It makes our work sustainable.

From Rescue to Responsibility

We often talk about "rescuing" children. But true rescue doesn't end when a child is removed from labour. True rescue ends when they're restored to a life of dignity, opportunity, and hope—and we've walked with them long enough to know they'll be okay.

In Gogunda, we saw how a quiet child became the voice that saved another.

That's what follow-up can do.

It plants seeds. It builds trust. And one day, that trust blooms into courage.

Let's not forget that final step.

Because when we follow up, we don't just protect one child.

We strengthen the whole system.

Highlights

This chapter serves as a powerful reminder that rescue alone is not enough. While initial interventions, identification, FIRs, shelter, counselling, and rehabilitation form the foundation of child protection, follow-up is what holds the entire structure together. From the writer's experience in field operations, one truth emerges consistently: children rescued from labour or trafficking remain vulnerable unless we stay with them after the formalities are over.

The chapter explores why follow-up is not a formality, but a lifeline. Without regular check-ins, children risk dropping out of school, returning to unsafe homes, or falling back into labour. Through a deeply personal story of a child rescued in Gogunda, which illustrates how trust built over months led the child to speak up and prevent another case of child marriage. Follow-up, in this instance, transformed a rescued child into a protector. The chapter outlines practical ways to institutionalize follow-up:

1. Minimum six-month monitoring with structured visits.

2. Coordination between teachers, NGOs, Anganwadi workers, and Childline.

3. Child-led goal setting and support for emotional recovery.

4. Tracking school integration and emotional well-being.
5. Early detection of signs of relapse such as silence, absenteeism, or mood changes.
6. Consistent documentation to ensure accountability.

More than a checklist, follow-up is positioned as a form of prevention. It helps avoid re-trafficking, re-exploitation, and emotional regression. It converts legal rescue into long-term recovery.

Even if the child is not from your familiar working area or from another state, you can still follow up through the network of CWC and NGOs working there. If you are associated with any department or government body, you can propose including the progress review of children at risk as an agenda item in the quarterly DCPU meetings of the concerned district.

Whenever I talk about working outside the area, there is a story in my mind which I have not been able to forget till date and it shows how the network is useful in other places for follow up and rehabilitation of children.

This case is not from some distant part of Rajasthan, not even from a nearby state, but from a place I had never even visited. It was during the pandemic, a time when communication was broken and travel was nearly impossible. I received information from the Jhunjhunu district about a case. A girl had been declared an adult and sold into marriage under a customary practice where women are bought and married from other parts of the country due to low gender ratio. Later, a case was registered against her, accusing her of running away after marriage and taking some jewellery with her. However, the reality was far more tragic. She managed to escape and was found crying outside a police station. She was presented before the SDM and sent to a Nari Niketan shelter home.

There, a woman officer who had worked on CNCP cases had once attended my training sessions, reached out to me. And said to me that she does not look like an adult at all; she looks like a child." When they spoke to the girl, she revealed that the name she had been given was not her real name. "I have been sold," she said. "I want to go back home. I am from Unnakoti district, Tripura." During the first lockdown, tracing her origins was almost impossible. The police had no record of her. Even through NCPCR, we found that no missing case had been registered from Tripura at that time.

This is where the strength of local NGO networks and persistent follow-up came into play. Despite the challenges of the lockdown, the teams did crucial groundwork and identified areas where, due to poverty, children were often taken away by traffickers under the false promise of a better future. It took over forty eight hours of continuous effort, but finally, we found the girl's family. Her mother admitted that her daughter had been taken away by traffickers, but they had not filed any report because they did not want to get entangled in the complications of an FIR. Meanwhile, the girl had been trafficked not once but five times, sold again and again during her harrowing journey from Tripura to Rajasthan.

At first, she was wrongly seen as the culprit. But once the truth surfaced, it became painfully clear that she was a victim in every sense. The Tripura High Court took cognizance of the case. She was flown back home by air, her dignity and rights restored. It was not just a rescue, it was a true rehabilitation. Her identity, childhood, and right to live freely were restored. Regular follow-ups were conducted through the Child Welfare Committee to ensure her well-being.

Chapter 12: Restoring Hope

With the hope that this will be a good start, the end of this book is dedicated to you.

I have shared with you the experiences and true incidents from my journey until from child labour rescue to rehabilitation. It is my sincere hope that these stories will not only prove useful to you but also guide you towards a meaningful direction.

Many times, when I am invited to give training on Child Labour, I begin with two slides. The first one shows a flowchart detailing how presently the rescue operations are being conducted

And then I present the second flowchart, one that combines everything we've discussed, a visual representation of what real rescue and rehabilitation should look like. This flowchart isn't just a tool; it's a roadmap built from the lessons learned through real-life struggles, and I hope it helps you understand how to navigate the complex world of child labour rescue and rehabilitation.

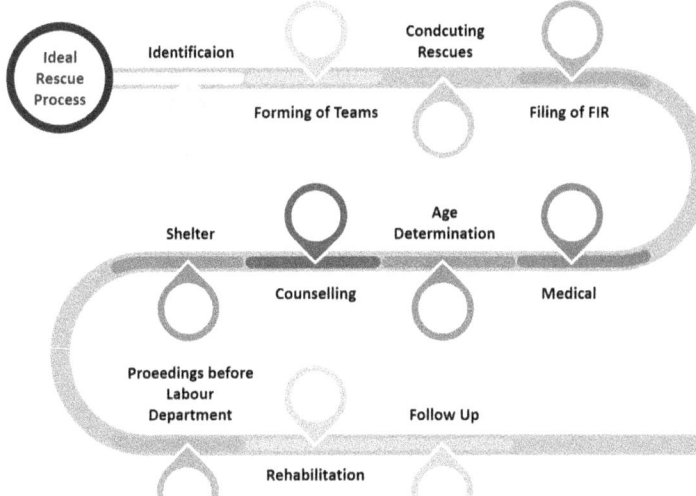

Most Inspiring Child Rights Activist of the Year at INDO-ARAB Leaders Summit in Dubai.

Samaj Ratan Award by Shri Ramesh Bais, Honorable Governor of Maharashtra.

'Desh Ratna Award' by the Shri Jagdambika Pal, Honorable Member of Parliament and former Deputy Chief Minister of Uttar Pradesh.

Leadership Excellence Award for Outstanding Contribution for Protection of Child Rights in India.

Invited as a speaker at TEDx.

'Social Change Makers' award by National Channel Doordarshan.

India's 100 under 40 'Social Leaders'

Peace Laureates Kailash Satyarthi and Leymah Gbowee

Awarded by Mr. Mahendrajeet Singh Malviya, then Cabinet Minister, GoR and then District Collector for commendable work in the field of child protection.

Awarded best social worker in All Media Council Awards at Constitutional Club, Delhi

Facilitated by Dr. Chinmay Pandya, Pro Vice Chancellor of Dev Sanskriti Vishwavidyalaya, All India Gayatri Pariwar

Relevant Information in Context of Child Labour

Constitutional Provisions Prohibiting the Employment of Children

Article 14: Equality before law, i.e. equal treatment and Protection under law. All children in similar circumstances are required to be treated in a similar manner, and if not so treated, such treatment can be challenged on the ground of discrimination and arbitrariness.

Article 15(3): Permits the State to make special provisions for women and children. Special enactments made for the benefit of children cannot be struck down on the ground of discrimination.

Article 19(1): Guarantees citizens of India the right to freedom of speech and expression, to form associations or unions, to move freely throughout the territory of India, etc. Under Indian law, child labour is prohibited only in factories, mines or other hazardous employment; therefore, there is no blanket ban on employment of children. Though children form part of the labour force they are not permitted to unionise and fight for their rights as workers

Article 21: This article guarantees the right to life to all persons. The Supreme Court has interpreted "right to life" to include the right to food, clothing, adequate shelter, and other basic necessities of life.

Article 21(A): The article 21A states that there must be a free and compulsory education to all children of age of six to fourteen years.

Article 22: Provides for safeguards upon arrest, and states that a person should be produced before the nearest Magistrate within 24 hours of arrest. A juvenile in conflict with law or a child in need of care and protection should be produced before the Competent Authority established under the Juvenile Justice [Care and Protection of Children] Act 2000 within 24 hours of having been picked up by the police.

Article 23: Prohibits trafficking in human beings and forced labour. Any contravention of this provision is punishable under law.

Article 24: Prohibits the employment of a child below 14 years in any factory or mine or any other hazardous employment.

Article 39(e) & (f): The State is required to ensure protection of children of tender age from abuse, and from entering vocations unsuited to their age and strength. Children are also to be provided with equal opportunities and facilities to develop in a healthy manner. The State is to further ensure that childhood and youth are protected against exploitation and abandonment.

Article 41: The State is required to take steps to secure Educational opportunities and facilities.

Article 44: The State is to endeavour to secure for all citizens a uniform civil code. A uniform civil code implies a uniform legal framework for adoption of a child applicable to all religions.

Article 45: The State is to take measures to ensure free and compulsory education for all children till they attain 14 years of age.

Article 47: The improvement of public health and the raising of the level of nutrition is a primary duty of the State.

Article 51(c): The State is to respect international law and treaty obligations. The Government of India and the State Governments are obligated to the commitments contained under the Convention on the Rights of the Child.

Major Legislative Measures governing Child Labour in India

Factories Act 1948

The Factories Act, 1948 prohibits the employment of a child below 14 years in any factory. To safeguard the health of young persons of above 14 years of age and below 18 years, and for their safety, the Act places a few other restrictions on their employment. Such young persons are required to obtain a certificate of fitness from a certifying surgeon. The Act also provides for initial and periodical examination (at intervals of not less than twelve months) of young person's by certifying surgeons. The Act puts restrictions on the working hours of these young persons. Thus, a child belonging to the age group of 14 years and below 17 years is not to be employed at night (night means a period of at least twelve consecutive hours which shall include the interval between 10 P.M. to 6 A.M.). Then a child between the age group of 14 and 15 cannot be employed for more than 4 ½ hours in any day, and he cannot be employed in two shifts and cannot be allowed to work in more than one factory on-the same day. Subject to what has been stated above, a young person between the age group of 15 years and 18 years is considered to be an adult for purposes of other provisions of the Factories Act, provided he has a certificate from a certifying surgeon that he is fit for a full day's work in a factory, otherwise he is considered to be a child.

MINES ACT, 1952

The Mines Act, 1952 has provisions regulating the employment of children in mines. The provisions in the Mines Act are more stringent than the Factories Act in this respect. No young person who has not completed the age of 16 years can be employed in any mine. A child (a person who has not completed 15 years of age) cannot even be present in any part of a mine which is below ground, and also above ground after such date as the central government may by a notification fix. A young person who is between 16 years of age and 18 (known as adolescent) is allowed to work in any part below ground if he has a medical certificate from a certifying surgeon certifying that he is fit for work as an adult. Even then such a person cannot be allowed to work at night.

EMPLOYMENT OF CHILDREN ACT, 1938

To prevent employment of children in hazardous occupations and those injurious to health, the Employment of Children Act, 1938 prohibits their employment in certain occupations. Thus, no child who has not completed 15 years of age can be employed in any occupation connected with the transport of passengers, goods or mails by railway; or a port authority within the limits of a port.

MERCHANT SHIPPING ACT, 1958

The Merchant Shipping Act, 1958 applies to sea-going ships. It has some provisions regulating employment of children. The Act bars employment in any capacity of a person below 15 years in a ship except (a) in a school ship, or training ship, in accordance with the prescribed conditions; or (b) in a ship in which all persons employed are members of one family; or (c) in a home-trade ship of less than two hundred tons gross; or (d) where such person is to be employed on nominal wages and will be in the charge of his father or other adult near male relative.

MOTOR TRANSPORT WORKERS ACT, 1951

The Motor Transport Workers Act, 1951 regulates the condition of work of employees in motor transport undertakings. Section 21 of the Act prohibits an employment of children in a motor transport undertaking, and a child is defined as a person who has not completed 15 years of age. An adolescent (a person who has completed 15 years of age but not 18 years) is allowed to work provided he has a certificate of fitness granted by a certifying surgeon. The certificate is valid for a period 0 of one year but can be renewed.

PLANTATION LABOUR ACT, 1951

The Plantations Labour Act, 1951 applies to plantations in tea, coffee, rubber or cinchona which measure 10.117 hectares or more, and in which thirty or more persons are employed Section 24 of the act prohibits employment of children. This act applies to any land used for cultivation of the coffee, rubber, cinchona or cardamom which measures five hectares or more and in which fifteen or more persons are employed.

CHILDREN (PLEDGING OF LABOUR) ACT, 1933

The Children (Pledging of Labour) Act of 1933 prohibits the making of agreements to pledge the labour of children for employment. A child is defined as a person who is under the age of fifteen years. An agreement to pledge the labour of a child is void under the Act. Such a contract will also be void under the Indian Contract Act on account of the contract being opposed to public policy.

APPRENTICES ACT, 1961

The Apprentices Act, 1961 regulates the training of apprentices in industry so that the programmes of training may be organised on a systematic basis, and the apprentices may get the maximum advantage of their training. The Act provides that a person who is less than 14 years of age will not be qualified for apprenticeship training. In other words only children between the ages of over 14 years and below 18 years adults are eligible for training.

SHOPS AND ESTABLISHMENTS ACT, 1961.

Different states have enacted their own statutes regulating conditions of work of workers in shops and establishments. These Acts apply to shops, commercial establishments, restaurants and work of workers in shops and establishments. These Acts apply to shops, commercial establishments, restaurants and hotels and places of amusement at notified urban areas, to which the Factories Act does not apply, the state governments are empowered to extend the application of the Act to such other areas or categories of establishments as may be considered necessary. The Acts prohibit the employment of a child in shops and establishments, and he cannot be employed even as a member of the family of the employer.

Generally speaking, a child is a person who has not completed the age of 12 years, though in a few states like Tamil Nadu, Pondicherry and Uttar Pradesh and even in Karnataka the age is 14 years.

CHILD LABOUR PROHIBITION AND REGULATION ACT, 1986 (AMENDMENT, 2016).

This Act may be called the Child Labour (Prohibition and Regulation) Amendment Act, 2016. In the Child Labour (Prohibition and Regulation) Act, 1986 (hereinafter referred to as the principal Act), for the long title, the following shall be substituted, namely:— An Act to prohibit the engagement of children in all occupations and to prohibit the engagement of adolescents in hazardous occupations and processes and the matters connected therewith or incidental thereto." According to this amendment Act "Child" means a person who has not completed his fourteenth year of age or such age as may be specified in the Right of Children to Free and Compulsory Education Act, 2009, whichever is more;' "Adolescent" means a person who has completed his fourteenth year of age but has not completed his eighteenth year. Under section 3 (1) of the Act, No child shall be employed or permitted to work in any occupation or process.

(2) Nothing in sub-section (1) shall apply where the child,—

(a) Helps his family or family enterprise, which is other than any hazardous occupations or processes set forth in the Schedule, after his school hours or during vacations;

(b) Works as an artist in an audio-visual entertainment industry, including advertisement, films, television serials or any such other entertainment or sports activities except the circus, subject to such conditions and safety measures, as may be prescribed:

Provided that no such work under this clause shall affect the school education of the child.

Section '3A' of the Act says that 'No adolescent shall be employed or permitted to work in any of the hazardous occupations or processes set forth in the Schedule.' According to section 14 (1) whoever employs any child or permits any child to work in contravention of the provisions of section 3 shall be punishable with imprisonment for a term which shall not be less than six months but which may extend to two years, or with fine which shall not be less than twenty thousand rupees but which may extend to fifty thousand rupees, or with both: Provided that the parents or guardians of such children shall not be punished unless they permit such child for commercial purposes in contravention of the provisions of section 3.

(IA) Whoever employs any adolescent or permits any adolescent to work in contravention of the provisions of section 3A shall be punishable with imprisonment for a term which shall not be less than six months but which may extend to two years or with fine which shall not be less than twenty thousand rupees but which may extend to fifty thousand rupees, or with both: Provided that the parents or guardians of such adolescent shall not be punished unless they permit such adolescent to work in contravention of the provisions of section 3A.

Landmark Judgement of Supreme Courts of India for Child Labour

Case Name	Year	Findings	Principal Rule Laid Down
M.C. Mehta vs State of Tamil Nadu	1996	Child labour stems from poverty and lack of opportunity. Focused on the unorganized sector.	Mandated Child Labour Rehabilitation Fund; Compulsory education and adult employment alternatives.
Bachpan Bachao Andolan vs UOI [WP (C) 51/2006]	2011	Recognized trafficking as organized crime.	Ordered total ban on child performers in circuses. Adopted UNCTOC's trafficking definition.
Bachpan Bachao Andolan vs UOI [WP (Crl) 75/2012]	2013	Concerned about missing children.	Mandated FIR registration for missing children. Directed SCPCR to use tech & SOP monitoring.
Bachpan Bachao Andolan vs UOI [WP (C) 906/2014]	2014	Rising substance abuse among children.	Directed Centre to complete survey and create national plan.
Bachpan Bachao Andolan vs UOI [WP (C) 558/2019]	2019	School safety concerns.	SC issued notices for enforcing child safety guidelines in schools.

Case	Year	Issue	Outcome
Society of Private Unaided Schools vs UOI & BBA	2012	Right to Education Act challenged.	Upheld constitutional validity of RTE Act, 2009.
Save the Child Foundation vs UOI [WP (Crl) 2069/2005]	-	Weak enforcement in child labour cases.	Directed rescue of 500 children/month, charge sheets in 45 days, compensation by DLSAs.
Bachpan Bachao Andolan vs State of Punjab [WP (C) 7565/2010]	2010	SOPs missing for child labour rescue.	Directed Punjab govt to draft SOP and action plan.
BBA vs State of Bihar [CWJC 11819/2010]	2010	Lack of policy implementation.	Ordered policy enforcement and officer training.
BBA vs State of Jharkhand [WP (PIL) 139/2011]	2011	Infrastructure gaps in child protection.	Ordered constitution of SCPCRs, CWCs, homes & JJ Act implementation.
Anaj Mandi Fire Case – BBA vs GNCTD	2023	Children died in an illegal factory fire.	Directed immediate rescue & rehabilitation. Emphasized Delhi Action Plan on Child Labour.
Manga vs State of Rajasthan	2022	Brick kiln trafficking and forced labour.	Directed police to recover children &

			prosecute traffickers.
Court on Its Own Motion vs Govt. of NCT of Delhi	2009	Poor enforcement of child labour laws.	Directed implementation of Delhi Action Plan for abolition of child labour.
Child Labour (Prohibition and Regulation) Act, 1986	-	Illegal employment of children.	Prohibits hazardous work for children under 14. Compensation for unlawful employment upheld by courts.
Hayathkhan vs Deputy Labour Commissioner	2005	Violations of Child Labour Act in Karnataka.	Upheld enforcement of child labour penalties.
BBA vs UOI [WP (C) 466/2016]	2016	POCSO-linked victim support issue.	Ordered release of Rs. 25 crores from Victim Compensation Fund.

Myths about Child Labour

Myth #1: If he doesn't work, how will he survive?

Reality: This is a common but harmful belief. Child labour actually worsens poverty instead of solving it. Education is the key to long-term survival and success. When children work instead of going to school, they lose the opportunity to gain essential skills for better jobs in the future. Working in hazardous conditions also damages their health, reducing their ability to earn in adulthood. To truly help families survive, adult wages must be increased so that children can attend school.

Myth #2: I worked as a child, and it didn't harm, so child labour isn't a real problem.

Reality: Child work and child labour are not the same. Child labour specifically means work that robs children of their childhood, damages their dignity, and limits their potential. It includes tasks that are mentally, physically, or emotionally harmful and that disrupt their education. Out of the 265 million children engaged in some form of work globally, around 168 million are involved in child labour that puts their health, safety, and future development at serious risk.

Myth #3: He is now the sole provider for the family.

Reality: While economic hardship may force children to work, it should not make them responsible for their families. This burden robs them of their childhood, education, and future potential. If adults are paid fairly and household incomes improve, families can survive without relying on children. Societies should focus on creating decent work opportunities for adults rather than normalizing child labour.

Myth #4 What good will studying and education do?

Reality: Education is fundamental for breaking the cycle of poverty. It equips children with skills and knowledge necessary for better-paying, safer jobs in adulthood. Without education, children are trapped in low-wage, exploitative work, often for life. Investing in education benefits not just individuals but the overall economy through higher productivity and innovation.

Myth#5 Most child labourers are nearly adults, so it's acceptable.

Reality: In truth, a large number of child labourers are very young. About 44% are between just five and eleven years old—around 77 million children. Of the 85 million involved in hazardous work, nearly 38 million are aged five to fourteen, with more than half under twelve. This highlights how deeply childhood is being stolen from these children, far earlier than many assume.

Myth #6 The day these people stop working, development will come to a halt.

Reality: This is factually incorrect. Child labour hinders economic growth, not supports it. Studies show a strong negative correlation between child labour and national income (GDP per capita). In other words, the more child labour exists, the lower a country's income and development tend to be. Child labour depresses wages, increases adult unemployment, slows technological advancement, and discourages foreign investment. Sustainable growth is achieved by investing in human capital by creating a workforce of educated and healthy adults, not by exploiting children. When children are forced into labour, nations miss out on building skilled and productive populations that are essential for long term economic success.

Myth #7 The family's work was always this; if they learn it early, it will benefit them more.

Reality: This belief confuses skills development with exploitative labour. Learning a family trade under safe, non-exploitative conditions while getting a proper education is fine. However, forcing children into hazardous, full-time work deprives them of schooling, stunts their development, and exposes them to physical and psychological harm. Early exposure to such harsh conditions harms rather than benefits children. Child labourers work in sweatshops.

Myth #8 They do menial jobs.

Reality: Studies show that most child labourers are found in the agricultural sector, Industries like factories, construction sites, and mines accounts for only about 7.2 percent of child labour. In contrast, nearly 58.6 percent of child labourers work on farms and plantations, deeper in the supply chain. These children engage in tasks like planting, cultivating, and harvesting raw materials such as cotton, which are later used in products sold worldwide. Agricultural child labour is particularly dangerous, exposing children to long hours of physically demanding work, toxic pesticides, and heavy lifting, all of which can seriously harm their health and development.

Myth #9 It is culturally acceptable.

Reality: In some places, child labour has become so common that it is seen as "normal." However, just because it is accepted in some cultures does not make it any less harmful to children or their communities. Research shows that when adult wages rise and household incomes improve, parents tend to pull their children out of the workforce, proving that child labour is not a cultural preference but often an economic necessity. Reducing child labour and increasing family incomes can create a ripple effect, helping new social norms emerge that reject child labour even further. Education is also crucial for breaking this cycle. When children are given the opportunity to learn, they grow up better equipped to make informed decisions and create a future where the next generation is protected from exploitation.

Myth #10: Children can continue their education after earning some money

Reality: Returning to school after working is far more difficult than it seems. Child labourers typically earn very little, much less than adult workers but poverty forces them into work to help their families survive. As a result, they are unlikely to save enough for future education. A more sustainable solution is for companies and governments to ensure that adult workers are paid fair wages, enabling families to prioritize education over child labour.

Moreover, children who leave school often struggle to catch up academically. Long hours of hazardous work can seriously impact their health, well-being, and cognitive development, leading to behavioural issues and learning difficulties that make it even harder to return to education and complete their studies successfully.

Myth #11: There will always be child labour, it's too big a problem to solve.

Reality: Child labour can be ended. Since 2000, the number of child labourers globally has dropped by one-third — meaning 78 million children have been freed from exploitative conditions. This progress is thanks to the combined efforts of governments, businesses, civil society, and individuals. However, much more work remains.

To keep this momentum, we must tackle both the "supply" of vulnerable children and the "demand" for cheap goods made through exploitation. Businesses must actively protect children throughout their workplaces, supply chains, and communities. They should also be transparent, report their actions to prevent exploitation, and seek independent audits of their labour practices. Ending child labour is possible — but it requires sustained, collective action.

Myth #12: Child labour only happens in poor countries.

Reality: Child labour is a global issue, not just a problem of poorer nations. While Africa, Asia, and the Pacific account for 9 out of 10 child labourers, millions of exploited children also live in the Americas and Europe.

In the United States, reliable data on child labour is scarce, but one fact is clear: between 2003 and 2016, 452 children died from work-related incidents. More than half of these deaths occurred on farms, where children, some as young as seven, often work 10-hour days. Gaps in U.S. labour laws leave child farmworkers especially vulnerable. Focusing only on child labour abroad risks ignoring the exploitation happening much closer to home.

Myth #13: Child labour helps young people transition into better paid jobs as adults.

Reality: Research shows that early involvement in child labour actually harms a young person's future employment prospects. According to the ILO's 2015 report, those who were child labourers are more likely to end up in unpaid family work or stuck in low-wage jobs as adults. Additionally, those who leave school before or at the minimum working age of 15 face a greater risk of being excluded from the workforce altogether. Rather than setting children up for success, child labour traps them in cycles of poverty and limited opportunity.

Supporting Child Protection Structures in India

List of Abbreviations

Abbreviation	Full Form
ASHA	Accredited Social Health Activist
AHTU	Anti-Human Trafficking Unit
CCI	Child Care Institution
CPC	Child Protection Committee
CWC	Child Welfare Committee
CNCP	Children in Need of Care and Protection
CWPO	Child Welfare Police Officer
DCPU	District Child Protection Unit
DLSA	District Legal Services Authority
FIR	First Information Report
GRP	Government Railway Police
ICPs	Individual Care Plans
IPC	Indian Penal Code
JJ Act	Juvenile Justice (Care and Protection of Children) Act
NCPCR	National Commission for Protection of Child Rights
NGO	Non-Governmental Organization
PLCPC	Panchayat Level Child Protection Committee
POCSO Act	Protection of Children from Sexual Offences Act
RPF	Railway Protection Force
RSCPCR	Rajasthan State Commission for Protection of Child Rights
SDG	Sustainable Development Goal
SJPU	Special Juvenile Police Unit
SOP	Standard Operating Procedure
TC	Ticket Collector
TTE	Train Ticket Examiner
UNCRC	United Nations Convention on the Rights of the Child

www.ingramcontent.com/pod-product-compliance
Lightning Source LLC
LaVergne TN
LVHW061616070526
838199LV00078B/7309